Personal Branding for Brits

by Jennifer Holloway

How to sell yourself to find a job and
get on at work...without sounding like an idiot

Published by

spark

SECOND EDITION – May 2014

Author: Jennifer Holloway
ISBN: 978 0 9575428 0 8
Copyright: © Jennifer Holloway, 2012

Published by:
Spark Ltd
2 Sandybeck Cottages
Skipton
North Yorkshire
BD23 3LD

www.sparkexec.co.uk

Designer: Mark Spanton, Captiva Design
Cover photography: Mark Ingram, MKI Photo

In memory of my stepdad Jim

To use his phrase, last time we saw him he was heading east.

WHY READ THIS BOOK?

Journalists. They can be a harsh bunch – hard to win over and with a string of other contacts to call if you don't manage to. I should know…I spent 15 years of my career responding to their varying requests, from my early days as a naïve press officer to the latter ones as a savvy media executive.

If ever there was a job where you needed to promote you, not just your company, that was it. You had to build relationships, get buy-in and stay on people's radars if you were to have any chance of standing out from the press office crowd. It didn't take me long to realise the only real differentiator I had was me…so I used it: every time I picked up the phone, every time I sent an email, every time I met someone in person. It worked and I got my stories (and me) on the front page of the national papers as well as on TV and radio – including *The Today Programme*, *BBC Breakfast* and *Sky News*.

I learnt to sell the 'who' before I even began to sell the 'what'. And it doesn't matter what you do (or want to do), you need to do the same if you're going to find a job, bag a promotion, start a business, land a new client, or just get ahead at work.

Which isn't to say I had the art of selling myself all wrapped up… far from it.

Whilst I had a knack for making people believe I was über-confident, in reality it was little more than a veneer of self-assurance. My wafer-thin armour would deflect doubt for weeks, sometimes months, then crack with the smallest of prods: a throw-away remark from a boss, a piece of well-meant feedback from a colleague, a mickey-take from a friend. People didn't see it but I'd go home and blub my eyes out. Then I'd pull myself together, patch up the armour and head back out again.

After a decade and a half of doing PR though, something clicked and I fell out of love with my job. As part of figuring out what had happened, I had some executive coaching and, as people often do, decided that was the career for me. I got my qualification, set up shop and started the long, challenging task of gaining and retaining clients. Every piece of work I pitched for was like a job interview: I had limited time to go in, sell the 'who', explain the 'what' and hope they liked what they saw. More intimidating was the fact I am my business, so getting buy-in to me was more essential than ever.

It worked and my business grew. However, not long in I realised I didn't want to be a little fish in a huge pond of thousands of coaches. I wanted my own puddle where I could do things my way and mark myself out as different. Looking at the issues I was helping clients with, I realised most led back to the fact the person lacked confidence. They didn't know who they were so they didn't know who to be or what to do. In other words they didn't know their personal brand. Bingo!

I reworked my whole business and started again, only this time I was selling something people weren't inclined to know about and were less inclined to buy – a pretty tough challenge.

I set to work defining my own brand in a way that I never had before, really thinking it through and focusing on all the great stuff I bring to the table. And an amazing thing happened...

I started spending a lot more time in the Land of Self-Confidence, a wonderful place where everything's rocking and rolling: you love what you do, other people love what you do and success is your best friend.

It's not my permanent residence though. I still take trips to the Land of Self-Doubt where nobody rates you and it's a dead-cert you're going to fail…you might know the place. But because I've got a road-map for the Land of Self-Confidence (my personal brand) I find it easier and quicker to get myself back there.

That's why I wrote this book – to give people a steer on how to create their personal brand and, just as importantly, get it out there so they can spend more time in the Land of Self-Confidence too. Or to put it another way, I want people to be more successful just by being themselves.

None of what you'll read in this book is rocket science. It's simply common sense stuff that tends to get forgotten as we go about our busy lives. So let's get on with refreshing your memory…

CONTENTS

INTRODUCTION

If you're a Brit reading this book – or from any other country where modesty rules – congratulations! You've already overcome the biggest cultural hang-up to your personal brand: that it's 'not the done thing' to have one, let alone tell anyone else you have one. After all, arrogance is not an attractive quality. So here's the good news: the book you have in your hands is especially written by a Brit (me) for Brits (you) to avoid the arrogance entirely and provide a guide to subtly blowing your own trumpet without sounding like an eejit.

HOW TO USE THIS BOOK

This book isn't just any old guide to personal branding, it's a practical guide. What that means is alongside the 'thinking bits' about what personal branding is and how it works sits a heck of a lot of tools and techniques to apply that thinking in the real world.

The book is set out in two parts: the first focuses on **Creating Your Personal Brand** by defining it (if you don't know what you're selling how can people buy it?) then checking how it's perceived by others (is what you're selling what people are buying?) The second part moves on to **Promoting Your Personal Brand** (because there's no point keeping a good thing to yourself) in three key places: in the office, out and about and online.

The first part – **Creating Your Personal Brand** – requires a bit of time and a lot of thinking, but if you're serious about your career or business I'd recommend starting there. However, if you've a pretty good idea of what your brand is already, feel free to skip straight to the second part – **Promoting Your Personal Brand**.

Whichever chapter you're reading, I've included lots of real-life examples to show you what I'm talking about, although some names have been changed to respect confidentiality. There's a round-up of Dos and Don'ts at the end of each section as a reminder. Plus you can always do what I do and write extra notes in the margin as you go along (don't worry, I won't tell the librarian).

THE PRIMARY RULE

By reading this book you've become part of the growing band of people who realise that hiding your light under a bushel is no longer the canniest thing to do: people who want to move their career to the next stage; people who realise they can't do their job until they've got buy-in from their team; people who understand their personal brand is their company brand; people who are leaders of tomorrow establishing their credentials today.

Whatever reason you have for wanting to work on your personal brand, they all lead back to one primary rule:

People buy people.

You may be nodding your head thinking, "Uh-huh, she's got that right." You may even remember times you've instantly clicked with someone or others when you were instantly turned off. It's a well-known phrase but there's a bit to add that often gets overlooked:

People buy people and it's your personal brand that tells them what they get when they buy you.

For a great example of that, think about salespeople. Sometimes you go into a shop not expecting to buy anything but walk out with a bag on your arm because they had a personal brand you liked. (I've got a raspberry coloured knitted coat for exactly that reason. Believe me, it looks a lot better than it sounds.) Other times you walk away without the thing you went in for because the person's brand didn't work for you.

Here's what I'm talking about...

My friend decided she was going to buy a new Audi A4 – sure as eggs is eggs. She drove to the nearest dealership, walked in, met the salesman and thought, "I am never going to buy a car from you." His handshake and tone of voice told her everything she needed to know about his personal brand...and she didn't buy it. So she got in her car, drove 12 miles to the next dealership and bought the A4 there.

That's people buying people in action, but it's not just reserved for salespeople – we're all 'buying' or 'not buying' people whenever we come into contact with them. When you consider how many people you've come into contact with over the course of your career or business, and how their buy-in (or lack of it) has affected your success, you start to realise the importance of a personal brand. Plus when you consider how many more people you'll come into contact with, and how their buy-in will affect your future success, you start to realise why working on your brand with the help of this book is a marvellous idea!

Here's what I'm talking about...

Let's pretend you work in an office (indeed, maybe you do) and 5pm has rolled around. You've got an urgent job to finish and really need some help, so you approach a colleague who's packed up for the day and is in the process of putting their coat on. When you tell them what you need, do they slide their coat off, put it back on the hook and say, "Let's get started"? (A sure sign they've 'bought' you.) Or do they hurriedly button up their coat, avert their eyes and walk away with some vague mumble about it being parents' evening and they're already late. (A sign they probably haven't.)

THE PAYBACK

As well as helping your career or business, here are 10 other ways you'll get payback from spending time on your brand:

1. Defining your personal brand gives you the confidence to be yourself.
2. Being yourself is a lot easier than trying to be someone else.
3. By focusing on what's great you add clarity to your brand.
4. You can pinpoint the thing that really makes you stand out from the crowd.
5. Promoting your personal brand helps you sell your benefits.
6. By selling the benefits people know what they're buying.
7. Doing this consistently helps people trust what they're buying.
8. People like to put things into neat little boxes in their mind, so you give them the box to put you in.
9. By having you in a neat box, it's easier for people to sell you and your benefits to others.
10. If you don't do it, you'll get left behind. Need I say more?

FINAL OBJECTIONS

If you're still thinking, "What the chuff do I need a personal brand for?" here are a few of the objections I've heard over the years, along with my response:

"It's not relevant to me."

If you have a job and think the only reason you'd promote your personal brand is to get another job, think again. Promoting your brand is what you need to do to ensure you keep the job you have. The same applies if you're the boss of your own business; you might think you can't be fired, but your clients can certainly go elsewhere.

"I'd be embarrassed to blow my own trumpet."

My advice: get over it. Modesty is indeed a virtue but you can take it too far and while you're busy being a shrinking violet, your colleagues and competitors are getting promotions and winning contracts that should have been yours.

"My work should speak for itself."

The days when hard work and determination would get you to the top are over. They are no more. They have ceased to be. This attitude is as useful as a dead parrot because everyone's so busy running to keep up they don't have time to pay attention to what you're doing.

Here's what I'm talking about...

After 15 years with the company, my client had recently been promoted to the Board, along with a colleague who'd been there only three years. He told me how unfair this was as, "John only got the job because he's good at blowing his own trumpet, but I think my work should speak for itself." My response was, "Really...how's that been working for you?" There's a balance between all style and all substance but the fact he'd taken five times longer to become a director suggested he'd got it wrong.

"I don't want people knowing everything about me."

Nor do they want to know. You decide which bits are worth shouting about and stick to those. And if you don't want people knowing you spend your spare time re-enacting The Battle of Hastings or building scale models of Big Ben out of matchsticks... don't tell them.

"I can't be bothered with all that."

Ever heard the phrase, "You snooze, you lose"?
Enough said.

BACK TO BASICS

I've already mentioned this book offers a practical guide to creating and promoting your personal brand, but before we knuckle down to the hard work, I thought a little bit of background would hit the spot. Having learnt never to 'ass' 'u' 'me' people know what I'm talking about (especially my other half) I'll start by going back to basics with what I mean by a personal brand.

As I said on page 12: people buy people and it's your personal brand that tells them what they get when they buy you. It's the complete package, the whole shebang, everything and the kitchen sink – and it works a lot like any other brand.

> ### *Here's what I'm talking about…*
> Imagine you're in the supermarket looking at shelf upon shelf of washing powders. Essentially, they all do the same thing: get your clothes clean. So how do you choose which one to put in your basket? Each powder has a brand, conveyed through its packaging, colours, typeface, advertising, etc that subliminally delivers messages about what else you'll get besides clean clothes. It might be 'I wash clothes and I'm kind to the environment'. It might be 'I wash clothes and I save you money'. It might be 'I wash clothes and they'll smell like a sea breeze'. Learning about the 'and' helps you identify the thing that matters most to you and, with it, which one to buy.

Your personal brand is there to achieve the same thing by selling the 'and' that makes you different from everyone else. Before we go any further though, let's look at what makes up a personal brand.

WHAT IS A PERSONAL BRAND?

Us humans are complicated creatures, aren't we (what with our conscious and subconscious, egos and super-egos)? When I started working with clients I soon realised I'd have to simplify all the things that make us tick into one easy-to-follow diagram to give people a way of defining themselves clearly and concisely. Here's what I came up with – the Personal Brand Pyramid:

(For anyone who remembers being taught *Maslow's Hierarchy of Needs* at school, yes, it looks a little familiar.) To explain a little more, here's a brief overview of the six elements that make up your personal brand, then we'll go much more in-depth later.

Values

Your Values are principles by which you live your life, the moral compass you use to define right and wrong. Think of them as the foundations upon which your personal brand is built.

Drivers

Your Drivers are what you hold to be important to you, the things that motivate you to do what you do, to be who you are, that push you to succeed.

Reputation

In a nutshell, your Reputation is what you're known for (or want to be known for), the thing you communicate so clearly people think of it the instant they hear your name.

Behaviours

Your Behaviours are what give you your personality and character. They're what you say and do as an outward communication of those deeper Values and Drivers.

Skills/Strengths

Your natural talents, the things you excel at, whether technical or behavioural, plus your knowledge and experience – these are your Skills and Strengths. And last, but certainly not least…

Image

Your Image is the packaging for your brand – how you look (your clothes, body language, eye contact), how you sound (your tone of voice, volume, language) and how you act. These provide the clues to the other five elements of your brand.

The top three elements in the pyramid are what I call the 'intangibles'; they're the emotionally-based, deep and meaningful stuff that deliver a lot but can be hard for others to get a handle on. The bottom three elements comprise the 'tangibles'; they're based on logic, in so much as people can readily see what you're wearing, hear what you're saying, tell what you're good at and experience your behaviour. Today, the emphasis for sharing your brand with others is shifting from the tangible levels to the intangible ones. To put it another way: these days the 'who' is just as important as the 'what'.

BUSINESS IS CHANGING

No real surprise there, we all know things change, but the difficult bit is realising what you need to do differently to keep up with that change. Let me give some examples of what I mean:

Change #1 – The job for life

As we know, the 'job for life' no longer exists. Now transience is the order of the day, moving around to progress your career. In fact, one survey by Execunet in 2012 revealed that corporate leaders are changing jobs every 3.3 years (lessening from 3.6 years in 2005).

Career planning is no longer just something you do when you're ready to move on, it's a constant process of keeping in touch, nurturing your contacts and sowing the seeds of opportunity in people's minds.

Change #2 – The 9 to 5 office day

Something else that doesn't exist any more is working in the office, 9am to 5pm. Now, you can be working on the train, in the coffee shop, at your kitchen table, before the kids go to school, after the kids have gone to bed – after you've gone to bed. Great as that is, it means you become less visible and if people don't see you around, they don't miss you when you're gone.

The challenge is to find ways to maintain a presence even when you're not in the office – to make sure people know the part you play. Which leads me to the next change…

Change #3 – Growth by profits

Companies are no longer looking to grow simply by making profits, they're looking to grow by making cuts – and that includes job cuts. So ask yourself this: when your boss is sitting with their list deciding who should stay and who should go, or your client is wondering which suppliers to ditch, what have you done to prove your worth?

How will they know you are an asset to their business and not just a commodity?

Change #4 – Reputation spread

Something else to consider is the viral nature of today's communications. Before, what went on in a company stayed in a company, but now people's reputations, good or bad, can spread worldwide at the touch of a button. That's why it's important to spend time building a positive reputation so, should something go wrong, you've got some credit in the bank to stand you in good stead.

Here's what I'm talking about...

An international survey by Burson Marstellar found that 50% of a company's reputation is directly linked to its CEO's reputation. It's something that Richard Branson, king of the personal brand, understands well. He spends time putting himself out there, building a positive reputation, so that when his companies hit problems (as they often do) he still gets reasonably favourable press. Compare that to Tony Hayward, the CEO of BP no-one had heard of before the 2010 oil disaster off the US coast, who had done nothing to build up any reputation credit. With no buy-in to his brand journalists found it a lot easier to rip him to shreds, even when what he was saying was fair comment.

Change #5 – Decisions based on logic

One final change – and the one that just keeps growing – is the amount of choice we have, which means making decisions a whole lot harder. In the old days, logic would take care of it. If two people were interviewed for a job and one had a qualification the other didn't, the qualified person was usually hired. Simple.

Now, every person is qualified, so logic won't cut the mustard. Instead we have to take our decision to a more emotional level, looking for a connection with the person themselves – do we like them, do we trust them, do we buy them? What's required today is to set out your stall not just with the value of your skills, but the emotional value you offer too. The stronger the emotional connection you can offer, the better the buy-in to your brand.

WHERE YOUR BRAND EXISTS

For the most part, this book is about defining and sharing what you want people to think about your personal brand. However, it's important to realise that your brand exists in two places:

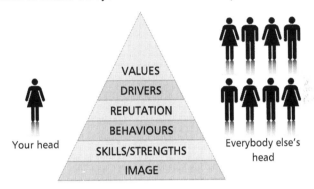

Your head

VALUES
DRIVERS
REPUTATION
BEHAVIOURS
SKILLS/STRENGTHS
IMAGE

Everybody else's head

It starts with a first impression that takes literally the blink of an eye. That's because, according to a study conducted by Janine Willis and Alexander Todorov at Princeton University in 2006, you need only one-tenth of a second to gather all the information necessary to suss someone out. Primarily, it's their trustworthiness that you're gauging, though the study also showed we quickly rate their attractiveness, likeability, competence and aggressiveness too.

Now, you may be thinking, "I've got a tenth of a second to work out all that...how the heck?!" It's a lot easier than you might think though because your brain's doing it without you even realising. Here's how:

When our brain experiences something for the first time, its primary need is to understand how to react to it. Specifically, the amygdala (a small part of your brain responsible for emotional response) is on stand-by to implement our fight, flight or freeze reaction. This goes back to prehistoric times when, if a caveman happened upon an animal, he had to quickly decide if it was something to eat (in which case to fight) or something that might eat him (requiring flight or freeze as a response).

To help decide the best course of action, our brain goes searching for clues. So when you meet someone for the first time, all five senses will be gathering data to feed your grey matter. You'll look for clues – an expensive watch could give you an idea of someone's wealth. You'll listen for clues – a regional accent could give you an idea of someone's upbringing. You'll feel clues – a firm handshake could give you an idea of someone's confidence. You'll smell clues – a strong whiff of cigarettes could give you a clue to someone's lifestyle. On the odd occasion, you may even taste clues (though licking people's faces isn't the best etiquette).

Once your brain has the clues, it sets about interpreting them using a 'reference library' it's built up based on a whole host of things including your family upbringing, memories and experiences, cultural stereotypes and even social expectations. You need to remember though, not everyone's libraries will be identical, so the same clue could be interpreted different ways. As the American writer EB White said, "Prejudice is a great time saver. You can form opinions without having to get the facts."

Here's what I'm talking about...

Let me tell you about my friend Emma Simpson-Duke. Actually... why don't you just take a second to imagine what she's like. Did you picture someone posh, wears a Hermés scarf to work (not that she needs a job, what with daddy's trust fund) and jodhpurs at the weekend, talks in a plummy voice and drives a natty little sports car? I did and before I even met her I knew exactly what to expect. Or at least I thought I did. What I actually got was a salt-of-the-earth girl from Plymouth, who'd gone to Hull Uni, had a filthy laugh, swore like a navvy and got the Tube to work. Certainly taught me a lesson.

Remember that whilst you're gathering clues about the person you've just met, they're doing exactly the same and bingo – your brand has been created in their mind. (And according to a study by Michael Sunnafrank at the University of Minnesota, the opinions we form in the first minutes play a major role in determining the course of the relationship.) It doesn't stop there though. People will carry on picking up clues every time they come into contact with you, building a clearer picture of your personal brand. So it's up to you to make sure you give yourself the best chance possible that people's perception of you is the one you want them to have.

YOU CAN'T PLEASE ALL THE PEOPLE

As a final bit of background, there's something important I want to share with you. Pay attention now, because this is the key to personal brand happiness:

Not everyone will buy your brand – accept it.

That's exactly as it should be because trying to make everyone a fan of your brand is like trying to get Madonna to act her age – you're on a hiding to nothing. I've seen people try though.

Here's what I'm talking about...

I was once delivering a workshop to a group of people who had never met before. When I got to the bit where each attendee shares their first impression of the others, one guy said, "We can't do this. If I'd have known we were going to be getting feedback I'd have come into the room entirely differently. I'm a chameleon and I change who I am to match the people I'm with." Needless to say, his credibility disappeared faster than a chocolate biscuit at a Weight Watchers meeting.

However, if you can embrace who you are – even the imperfections – you can be successful just by being yourself.

Here's what I'm talking about...

In the early days of my business, the first personal brand I worked on was mine. I spent many hours honing and tweaking it and, once I was happy I had the best version of me down on paper, I moved on to the next stage: getting feedback.

I drew up a list of people whose opinions I valued – ex-bosses, colleagues and clients – then sent them questions asking what their perceptions of my brand were, so I could match them with my own. The answers rolled in, some of which made for great reading. Finding out I was seen as "immune to the temptation of following the majority" and "the person who makes stuff happen" was a real confidence boost. Others hit a nerve, like the one that said, "You have a strong style, like double espresso, but sometimes I wanted tea."

When I read that I was mortified because it highlighted all the things I knew to be my weaknesses – being too full on (not just a single but a double espresso), not listening (I hadn't even known they'd wanted tea) and having all the subtlety of a brick (aka "a strong style"). I went to bed and cried, blubbing to my other half that I may as well quit now because no-one would ever buy my brand.

When I woke next morning the very first thing I did was go straight back to that email to re-read the comment and beat myself up a bit more (admit it...you'd probably do the same).

Then it hit me...

If you had to come up with a metaphor for the brand I'd just spent weeks defining, double espresso would fit the bill, so the perception of my brand was spot on. The fact this person wanted tea didn't really factor into the equation; I'd never been anything other than coffee with them because that was what they'd bought in the first place. And adding tea to the menu wasn't an option (it's just not who I am). What was most liberating though was realising I didn't have to – I could just continue being who I am.

That person did me a huge favour and ever since I've made sure the fact I'm a coffee person comes across loud and clear, from the way I dress to the design of my website, the blogs I write to the workshops I deliver, the picture on my profile to the biography that goes with it. That added clarity has led to a lot more coffee fans buying my brand and for those who find double espresso a bit full-on, I've accepted it's nothing personal – I'm just not their cup of tea (pun intended).

PART 1: CREATING YOUR PERSONAL BRAND

YOUR SIGNATURE DISH

Now you know the six elements that make up a personal brand and you understand why you can't not have a brand, it's time for the hard work: you're going to start thinking about what your own personal brand is.

To help explain what we're going to do, think of yourself as a chef who's trying to create a signature dish – something that, out of all the dishes you can cook, showcases your talent with only a few key ingredients (just like your brand). To do that, you need to follow a five-step process so let's get cracking with the first one...

Like any chef, you need to know what ingredients you have at your disposal before you can write your recipe. So put your pinny on because it's time for us to have a rummage in your pantry.

This exercise is all about making you think long and hard about who you are and what makes you tick, writing down your answers along the way. (You'll need paper and something to write with, unless you're less old-school than me, in which case get your iPad out.)

What follows is a series of questions, covering each of the six brand elements, aimed at really getting you thinking. You may not always come up with an answer, but you'll increase your chances if you can put aside some quality time to get your brain in gear. For some of my clients, that's been while sitting on a sun-lounger on holiday, away from the day-to-day stuff that could hinder their thinking. For others it's been the opposite; they've gone into the office early to get into a business frame of mind before answering. The important thing is to find the time and place where you do your best thinking because the better the ingredients at this stage, the better the final dish.

WHAT TO DO: Get thinking

Start with whichever of the six elements you want to tackle first (some people find it easier to begin with the intangible levels like Values and Drivers, others with the more tangible things like Behaviours and Image). Read each of the corresponding questions in turn, spending time thinking about each one in detail.

As you're creating your brand to help you with your career or business, keep in a professional, rather than personal, frame of mind when you're answering. Really let your brain off the leash and write down whatever comes into your head, whether it's individual words, phrases or sentences, whether they're positive or negative. So long as they get out of your head and onto the page, you'll keep your thinking moving.

Keep going until you can't come up with anything else for that question, then move on to the next one. Don't worry if you read a question and your mind goes blank – we all process information in different ways, so some questions may suit you better than others.

Finally, to show you I'm not a heartless task-master cracking the whip to overload your brain, at the end of each set of questions you'll find examples of ingredients you can either pinch or use to spur your thinking on again. It's OK if your answers don't match the ones listed (maybe you've come at the questions from a different angle) just keep on thinking. And we're off!

Values

Your Values form the cornerstone of your personal brand and are unlikely to change significantly as you make your way through life; they're what made you who you are and set the path for everything that follows. Ask yourself:

Q: What Values do I hold?

Q: What sets my moral compass?

Q: How do I decide what is right and what is wrong?

Q: What forms the basis of my choices in how I live my life?

Q: What do I strongly believe in?

Q: What characteristic or behaviour do I dislike in others?
   (Looking at the opposite can point to a Value you hold strongly.)

A note about that last question: sometimes it helps to use a bit of reverse psychology in your thinking, looking for the worst thing to give you a signpost to the best. For instance, if someone has said they'll ring me back by 4pm and it's now well into the evening with no word, that gets me spitting feathers because delivering on a promise is my #1 Value (the exact opposite of what's happened). Or I know plenty of people who, if they hold a door open for someone who walks through without saying "Thank you", find themselves muttering a sarcastic "You're welcome!" That's because courtesy and respect come pretty high on their Values list.

Here are some examples of Values:

- Honesty
- Community
- Independence
- Generosity
- Integrity
- Responsibility
- Loyalty
- Self-belief
- Acceptance
- High standards
- Caring
- Freedom
- Gratitude
- Dignity
- Courtesy
- Fairness

- Compassion
- Equality
- Empathy
- Humility
- Authenticity
- Consistency
- Faith
- Pride
- Open mindedness
- Obedience
- Harmony
- Commitment
- Duty
- Trustworthiness
- Fun
- Charity
- Modesty
- Philanthropy
- Justice
- Respect
- Selflessness
- Ethical

Drivers

To be truly happy in your work, it's important that your Drivers are being nurtured; getting what you need from what you do is what makes you a happy bunny. But when your Drivers aren't met, no amount of effort can make you truly enjoy your job.

There's a close tie between your Values and Drivers so it's fine if you get a bit of crossover. (In fact, you may find the same ingredients appear again and again throughout this exercise, which is fine.) Usually the latter comes from the former and as an example of the difference, honesty could be your Value and doing the right thing could be your Driver (it's how the honesty manifests itself). Or independence could be your Value and doing things your way could be your Driver. Now ask yourself:

Q: What motivates me and 'floats my boat'?
Q: What matters to me about what I do?
Q: Why do I do what I do for a living?
Q: What matters to me about who I am?
Q: When I'm happy in my work, what need is being met?
Q: If I think about a time when I was unhappy in my work, what was missing?

And one last question that can really help you get to the nub of your Drivers...

Q: What am I scared of?

Here's what I'm talking about...

I was filling in a questionnaire about fear one day (as you do) and 'What are you scared of?' was the starter for 10. After the flippant part of my brain replied, "Finding we've drunk the last bottle of wine," I got to thinking seriously. The first answer I came up with was, "I'm scared of going backwards," because having put in a lot of hard work growing my business, the last thing I'd want is for it to shrink again. But that didn't quite encapsulate it, so I thought, "I'm scared of not going forwards" – a subtle difference but an important one. But it still wasn't right, so I pushed my brain to find the exact words to express my fear: "I'm scared of not going forwards fast enough." Pinning that down helped me realise I'm only ever happy when I'm making progress and to do that I have a huge need to paddle my own canoe (my key Driver). That way I can go in the direction I want, at the speed I want, without anyone else sticking their oar in.

Here are some examples of Drivers:

- Do my best for myself
- Do better than others
- Earn a high salary
- Get to Board level
- Do the right thing
- Be myself at all times
- Make a difference to others
- Tell the truth at all times
- Nurture others' potential
- Deliver the unexpected
- Work with the 'best in class'
- Seek new adventures
- Job security for me
- Security for my family
- Do things my way
- Find personal contentment
- Never stop learning
- Run a FTSE 100 company
- Gain full qualifications
- Freedom to make decisions
- Never give up
- Grow my business
- Job security for my staff
- Follow my faith

- Put others first
- Work hard to play hard
- Have high calibre clients
- Challenge the norm
- Don't settle for second best
- Deliver the highest standard
- Leave a legacy for others
- Be seen as an industry leader
- Constant improvement
- Make my client happy
- Take risks others won't
- Become the 'go to' person

Reputation

We'll cover Reputation in a lot more detail in the part where you check your brand, but for now this is all about what you want your Reputation to be. It might be for something you've already achieved or something aspirational, though you should only consider the latter if it's something you can feasibly achieve. (For example, there's zero use me wanting to be known as someone who's reserved and reflective…it ain't gonna happen.)

Remember that you can actually have a Reputation for any of the other elements of your brand: a Value you hold, a Driver that motivates you, a Behaviour you exhibit, a Skill you're totally ace at or an Image that marks you out. Now ask yourself:

Q: What am I known for?
Q: What comment is made when my name is mentioned?
Q: What do I want to be known for that's feasible and achievable?
Q: What would I like people to say about me when I'm not in the room?
Q: What would I hate to have said about me?
    (Then look at the opposite of that to see what really matters.)

Here are some examples of Reputations:

- Always delivers on time
- Tells it like it is
- Thinks outside the box
- Finds the answer every time
- Keeps the team together
- Quick decision maker

- Creates order from chaos
- Spots the opportunities
- Dresses to impress
- Trusted by all
- Puts others first
- Loyal to the company
- What you see is what you get
- Life and soul of the party
- Brings something new
- No promise without delivery
- Stands up for the little guy
- Worth listening to
- A flamboyant personality
- Entirely authentic
- Connector of people
- Adventurous and risk taking
- Engaging communicator
- Sees all sides of the story
- Calm in a crisis
- Mathematical brain
- Always sees the silver lining
- Naturally funny
- People magnet
- Independent thinker
- The client's best friend
- Delivers on the bottom line
- Loves the tough challenges
- Has an inner serenity
- Respectful of others' views
- Holds people accountable
- Makes complex things simple
- Gets things off the ground

Behaviours

Now we're getting to the part where your personality comes to the fore – the 'who' that sits alongside the 'what'. Your Behaviours are the things that, even if you were dressed in a uniform doing exactly the same thing as the person next to you, would mark you out as different. Think about:

Q: What words would I use to describe your personality?
Q: What words would I use to describe how I act around others?
Q: What words would I use to describe how I behave?
Q: If I had three adjectives to describe me, what would they be?

Here's what I'm talking about...
Often there'll be one word that fits you to a tee – better than similar words in the same ballpark that don't quite feel right. When one client described herself as 'happy', I asked if that was it or whether perhaps she was 'joyous' or 'cheerful' or 'upbeat' or 'lively' or 'smiley' – at which point she stopped me and said with a beam, "Smiley...that's me!"

Here are some examples of Behaviours:

- Positive
- Serious
- Reserved
- Self-assured
- Calm
- Dependable
- Laid back
- Young at heart
- Reflective
- Sparky
- Inclusive
- Assertive
- Bold
- Diligent
- Diplomatic
- Witty
- Sunny
- Steady
- Joyful
- Fearless
- Independent
- Caring
- High-energy
- Peaceful
- Polite
- Dynamic
- Persistent
- Bubbly
- Resilient
- Composed
- Driven
- Open book
- Demure
- Sincere
- Charming
- Firm
- Graceful
- Spiritual
- Inspirational
- Spontaneous
- Dogged
- Adventurous

Here's what I'm talking about...

Take care to choose the right ingredient. A client had described herself as 'straightforward' but when I asked if that meant she was open, up front and 'what you see is what you get' she said, "Oh, no, that's not me. I often play my cards close to my chest." After trying (and failing) to pin down what she really meant by 'straightforward', we decided to move on with our discussions. A short while later she used the phrase 'matter of fact' to describe herself. When I queried what that meant she said, "Ah, this is what I was talking about earlier. I play my cards close to my chest because I like to gather the facts, so that when I do reveal them people know what I've said can be entirely trusted."

Skills/Strengths

For many people this is the easiest element to come up with answers for – what you're good at (or more specifically what you're great at). It's the stuff you'd readily talk about in an interview because you're confident in your abilities. Don't forget though that Skills and Strengths aren't just the things on your CV – they can be derived from other elements of your brand too, like your Behaviours or Values. So ask yourself:

Q: What am I great at?

Q: What comes naturally to me that might not come so easily to others? (Think of those times you've been asked, "How do you do that?" and replied, "I'm not sure...I just do.")

Q: What am I renowned for that people come to me for help with?

Q: What talent or technique have I made little or no effort to learn?

Q: When time flies and I'm enjoying my work, what am I doing?

Q: When I'm around a table with my peers, what's the thing I can do better than anyone else?

Here are some examples of Skills and Strengths:

- Lateral thinking
- Engaging writing
- Extracting key points
- Plate spinning
- Creating order from chaos
- Leading from the front
- Identifying cost savings
- Never ever give up
- Streamlining processes
- Never miss a deadline
- Create harmony in a team
- Natural charisma
- Authoritative
- Researching new concepts
- Revolutionary ideas
- Ask 'how', not just 'what'
- Quick witted
- Effortlessly funny
- Unerring focus
- Up to the minute
- Calm in a crisis
- Intuitive empathy
- Technologically savvy
- Spelling and punctuation

- Photographic memory
- Network building
- Persuasiveness
- Stress-testing ideas
- Engendering loyalty
- Creating top teams
- Quickly building rapport
- Help build others' careers
- Thinking beyond the norm
- Artistic eye
- Knowledge sponge
- Predicting trends
- Minutely detailed
- Communicating complexity
- Big picture vision
- Mediating conflict
- Project chunking
- Pinpointing problems
- Finding hidden agendas
- Having a way with words
- Generating energy in others
- Picking up a vibe
- Evaluating options
- Delegation
- Overcoming opposition
- Playing the game
- Naturally trustworthy
- Shoulder to cry on

If you're really struggling to figure out your natural talents, I can recommend investing in a copy of *Strengthsfinder 2.0* by Tom Rath. The book is built around the premise that we work best when we're playing to our strengths. To clarify what those strengths might be Gallup, the organisation behind the book, used years of research to create a list of 34 strengths people can have. Gallup then created an online survey to identify people's top five strengths, giving them a personalised report to explain how those work in day-to-day life and how they can be used for best effect in the future. (To take the survey you need a code that comes with the book, so always buy a new copy.)

Image

Whether you like to dress it up or keep it casual, people will be taking a keen interest in your Image – not just how you look (from your clothes to your body language) but how you sound as well (from your words to your tone of voice). Bear in mind your Image is the packaging that conveys the other five elements of your brand, so it needs to be cohesive and consistent to work. Now ask yourself:

Q: What words would I use to describe how I look?

Q: When I get dressed for work, what am I trying to convey with my clothes?

Q: What clues could someone pick up about me just from looking?

Q: What words would I use to describe my voice?

Q: What words would I use to describe how I communicate (including listening)?

Q: What words would I use to describe my body language (including eye contact)?

Here are some examples of Image:

- Classic
- Trendy
- Sharp
- Tailored
- Loud
- Understated
- Co-ordinated
- To the point
- Natural
- Polished
- Larger than life
- Youthful
- Colourful
- Vintage
- Open
- Articulate
- Down to earth
- City
- Subdued
- Flirty

- Chic
- Bold
- Elegant
- Conservative
- Dynamic
- Fast
- Soft
- Distinct
- Uniform
- Dramatic
- Outspoken
- Traditional
- Quirky
- Storyteller
- Low-key
- High-brow
- Unconventional
- Healthy
- Bright
- Energetic

How did you do? If you've got this far and your list of ingredients is as short as Ronnie Corbett's trouser leg, you may find it useful to spend a bit more time mulling things over.

That hour you spend journeying to work? Use that. The 20
minutes extra snooze time you clock up on your alarm? Use
that. The five or 10 minutes you spend in the shower? Use that.
This exercise isn't something to be rushed, so enjoy the novel
experience of thinking about yourself for once and not just the
daily routine.

ADDING SOME MEAT TO THE BONES

Was dredging your cupboards an easy experience? You'd think
it would be, because no-one knows you better than you do, but
many people struggle to put who they are into words because it's
alien to our everyday lives.

There's more thinking to come though because, while the
ingredients on your list may be good ones, there's every chance
they could be better. (And as I said before, the better the
ingredients, the better the final dish.)

Remember, your personal brand is about defining what makes you
stand out from the crowd and often it's the 'shades of grey' that
differentiate you from the next person. Adding meat to the bones
of your existing answers adds more definition to your brand. That
means you better understand what you're selling, and others have
a more specific idea what they're buying.

Here's what I'm talking about...
I asked Kate what three words she would use to describe herself.
The first was 'honest', which lots of people choose, so I quizzed her
more. She said it was a feeling she got in the pit of her stomach
when she felt she wasn't being true to herself, that would stop her
from doing something even if it meant she might lose out. Contrast
that to the many other definitions of honesty I've heard – everything
from 'not telling a lie' to 'following the rules' – and you start to see
some individuality appear.

This exercise is about using questions to challenge your thinking and ensure your ingredients really get to the nub of who you are. (You can stick with your existing list of ingredients and simply add any new answers onto the end.) There are two things you might find helpful – although they're not imperative. The first is a copy of *Roget's Thesaurus* to suggest alternative words/ingredients for the ones you have. (As opposed to *Roger's Profanisaurus* that potty-mouthed *Viz* readers will be familiar with.)

The second is someone to ask the questions – like being in the hot seat on *Mastermind* – because having to say your answer out loud means your brain can't skive off and think about something else. (It's something my clients say makes all the difference, so get in touch if you'd like me to challenge your thinking.)

WHAT TO DO: Keep thinking

Go back through your ingredients, reading each one in turn, and think about whether that one word or phrase is really doing justice to what you're all about; does it explain deeply enough the specifics of what makes you tick?

If you're someone who has hit the nail on the head first time and already has detailed answers, you can skip this bit. If not, ask yourself more questions (or get the person helping you to ask) to dig deeper into what you really want to say. A good one to start with is:

Q: What do I really mean by [ingredient]?

Depending on your answer, you could then follow that up with another relevant question, like one of these:

Q: Why am I [ingredient]?

Q: What makes me [ingredient]?

Q: What matters about [ingredient]?

Q: What am I aiming to achieve when I [ingredient]?

Q: What do I get from [ingredient]?

Q: What does my [ingredient] give others?

Q: How do I use my [ingredient]?

Q: How does my [ingredient] differ from others with that?

Q: Is there a better word to describe my [ingredient]?

Write down your new answers and like a toddler who always wants to know "Why?" keep going with the questions until you feel you've hit upon exactly the right words. If you've got help, here's an example of how a conversation might go:

- "You've put as an ingredient 'approachable' – what do you mean by that?"
- *"Well, I mean people find me friendly because I smile a lot and am quick to make eye contact."*
- "What makes you smile and make eye contact?"
- *"It's because I want people to know I'm genuinely interested so we quickly get into a conversation."*
- "What do you get from having a conversation?"
- *"I like to build rapport because that's how you find out about people – particularly what they're good at or have to offer."*
- "What does finding out what people have to offer give you?"
- *"It gives me a chance to spot opportunities – especially when it comes to hiring people to be part of my team."*
- "What matters about hiring people for your team?"
- *"I like to work with only the best people so we can produce the best work."*
- "So instead of just saying you're approachable, your ingredients should be 'show genuine interest in others', 'find out what they have to offer', 'spot opportunities', 'hire talented people' and 'create the best team to produce the best work'.

All you have to do now is repeat that for each ingredient. That could take some time (you'd best put *Masterchef* on to record) and a bit of effort, but once you get going you'll soon find yourself coming up with the same ingredients (or a variation thereof) so things will speed up. That's a good sign because it means you're identifying some strong themes for your brand and that you're really starting to get to the heart of the matter, which will make the next bit even easier.

AVOID THE BUFFET

By now you should have a fair few ingredients on your piece of paper/electronic device and it's probably starting to look a little overwhelming – I mean, who knew you were such a complicated old soul?

The good news is you're now a step closer to defining your personal brand (hooray!) However, because you're aiming for an á la carte dish, not a full-on smorgasbord, there's some more work to do paring down your ingredients.

This exercise is about making sure you use only the best ingredients for your final dish – what some people might call 'the dog's proverbials'.

The hard part is knowing what to leave out – after all, every ingredient on that list is pertinent or you wouldn't have put it on there. When I'm working with clients I use my knack for spotting a story to zoom in on their standout components and zone out the rest. (If you're really struggling to pare your ingredients, it's a service I offer, so give me a call.)

Whatever you do, avoid keeping too many on your list because you run the risk of switching people off from buying your brand at all.

Here's what I'm talking about...

Columbia University published a research paper called *When Choice is Demotivating* detailing an experiment it had run in a supermarket offering shoppers the chance to sample different flavoured jams. On the first day there was a choice of six jams to taste and anyone who did so was given a money-off voucher to use if they went on to buy one. The exercise was repeated with a choice of 24 different flavours of jam (four times as many) and the same number of vouchers were given out. When the researchers calculated how many vouchers were redeemed at the till, they found that when people had only half a dozen choices of jam, 30% went on to buy a jar. However, when the shoppers had 24 options only 3% made a purchase. Too much choice was demotivating and their brains switched off from the buying decision.

So like a holidaymaker packing their suitcase with only 10 kilos of luggage allowance, tough decisions have to be made (ditch the bottle of Ambre Solaire or the inflatable lilo?) Here's how to do it...

WHAT TO DO: Ask yourself the questions

Gather together your ingredients once more and with pen in hand (or keypad at the ready) go back through your list. For each one ask yourself the four questions that start on the next page, then take the appropriate action:

- If the ingredient elicits a "Yes" in answer to a question, it stays on your list.

- If the ingredient leads you to shout "Hell yes!" then not only does it stay on the list, but you should get out your highlighter pen and turn it a nice shade of yellow.

- If the ingredient leaves you thinking "Hmmm, not sure" then it's unlikely to be a strong contender so you might want to put a question mark next to it for now.

- If the ingredient has you answering with a firm "No" put a big, fat line through it (or hit delete). Of course, this doesn't mean you stop 'being' that ingredient – you haven't changed who you are with the strike of your pen – it just means it goes into the background for the purposes of your personal brand.

Now on to the questions:

Q: Is it a real strength?

The over-arching rule for an ingredient to stay on your list is that it has to be a real strength. One way of looking at it is to imagine yourself in a room with your peers – people at the same education, career, knowledge, experience and ability level as you. Now ask yourself whether, compared to everyone else, that ingredient is one you have in spades, for which you know you'd be among the best (if not the best) around the table.

Here's what I'm talking about...
Mike Pegg is the founder of www.thestrengthsfoundation.org. He defines your strengths as the ones that come naturally to you, that are effortless and that you enjoy – things you'd get an 'A' for on your school report. These are different from the things you'd get a 'B' or even an 'A-' for as those tend to be the things that come less naturally or you've had to teach yourself to be good at. There's a subtle difference between the two, so keep focused on ingredients that put you top of the class.

Q: Is it more than is expected?

A good example of an ingredient people often list is 'professional', but shouldn't being professional be expected (even if we can think of plenty of people who aren't)? You'd be wasting precious space in your personal brand if you included it. Another example is the ingredient from the conversation in the previous exercise: 'approachable'. Being approachable should be a given – it's the least people should expect from you – so ditch that ingredient and concentrate instead on the words that better illustrate what that means.

What's expected can also be specific to your job: an accountant who is 'good with numbers', a designer who is 'creative', a counsellor who is 'a good listener', a doctor with a 'knowledge of medicine'…it should be the least they do.

Q: Is it fresh and not just a cliché?

Your personal brand should make you stand out from the crowd, but if you end up using the same words everyone else is using, you'll be about as individual as a cloned sheep. Clichés tend to arise when a word or phrase that was once perfectly suitable becomes overused; while it's good to be things like 'strategic', 'creative', 'passionate' or 'innovative', the overuse of these buzz-words has resulted in their batteries running low and their impact reduced to a mere hum. If that's the case with your ingredient, then it's time to reach for the *Thesaurus* again to see if you can freshen it up a bit.

Q: If it disappeared from your list would you feel like a big chunk of who you are had gone?

This question is aimed at people for whom paring down their ingredients is more of an exercise in gut feeling than cold logic. Bottom line: if you read a particular ingredient and it 'just feels right' then by all means keep it in. If your reaction is a shrug of the shoulders and a grunt of "Meh" then take it out. Simples. Right, nearly there…

After all that – writing a list, building it up, paring it down – you should now have ingredients that represent the crème de la crème of who you are and what makes you tick. (I hope so or you'll be stymied when it comes to creating the final recipe for your signature dish!)

But before you can do a Delia/Nigella/Jamie/Heston/[insert name of your favourite chef here] you need to read the next, very important bit of this book.

MIRROR, MIRROR ON THE WALL

There's a line from the film *Chariots of Fire* that my father likes to quote when he manages people who, shall we say, are missing certain attributes that one would think necessary in business:

"I can't put in what God left out."

I'm reminded of this when I come across people who are ignorant of the fact they have a personal brand and, more importantly, the negative impact it's having. The attribute they're missing is the cornerstone of understanding who you are: self-awareness.

I've come across numerous people who seem to be blindfolded to others' reactions, or have cotton wool in their ears so don't hear people's jaws hitting the floor when they say or do something wholly inappropriate. But as the self-awareness was obviously never put in, there was never any chance it would come out.

Here's what I'm talking about...
Interviews are a great place to find people lacking self-awareness, like the lady who'd applied for a receptionist's position then chewed gum throughout our discussion. Or the guy who was meeting his friend after his interview and decided to text him while the questioning was in full swing to arrange the details. Or the woman whose phone rang during the interview and decided to answer it, before asking the interviewer to leave the room as it was a personal call.

Here's what you need to be asking yourself:

Q: What's my level of self-awareness?
Q: How much attention do I pay to people's reactions to me?
Q: Do I really know what people say about me when I'm not there?
Q: How could what they're saying be affecting my career/
business?

That last question is pretty much the crux of what I'm talking about. As I've already said on page 21 your brand exists in two places: in your own mind and in everybody else's. So even though you now have your list of ingredients as you see them, you need to make sure they're also how others see them before you can move forward. If you think your signature dish is shaping up to be a bottle of Dom Pérignon and a tin of Beluga caviar but others liken you more to a can of Vimto and a bag of pork scratchings, you'll be in for a hard time when it comes to getting buy-in for your brand.

So now's the time to do some market research to find out what your colleagues and peers are thinking. (Don't worry, I'm not asking you to stand in the street with a clipboard.)

IT'S NORMAL TO FEEL SCARED

If the prospect of finding out what others think makes you feel uncomfortable, congratulations: you've just proved you're human. In all my years of gathering feedback on my clients' brands and delivering the subsequent report, I've never found anyone who didn't have at least a little wobble in their stomach just before they got the results. It's normal and entirely understandable because what you're doing is putting yourself out there to be judged.

The good news is you can be pretty sure you'll get tons of really encouraging feedback – like an X Factor audition where Cheryl Cole says you're "purely belter". In 95% of the feedback reports I've delivered to clients that's absolutely the case.

Of course, you could also get comments more akin to Simon Cowell saying you're "tone deaf and talentless", which is less positive. And occasionally I've had to deliver reports with an element of that too.

Here's what I'm talking about...

One director whose feedback I delivered had his eyes opened by people's responses. In a lot of ways, his brand perception and theirs matched: he said he was focused, they said he was driven; he said he had a great business head, they said he was shrewd. But there was one area where their views diverged: whilst he saw his use of humour in the Boardroom as motivational, they saw him as a superficial smart-arse. He was taken aback. A huge part of his brand was that he was a fun guy, but it turned out he was seen as a bit too much of a joker. It was a positive experience though because, armed with that knowledge, he was able to tone down his antics (but not so much that he stopped being himself) and gain the respect he deserved.

Either way, it's better to know what people think than to go around believing you're the reincarnation of Elvis when you're more of a talent-show reject. Sticking your head in the sand won't change the fact your brand is being talked about in your absence because everybody – and I mean everybody – has a comment that gets added whenever their name is mentioned.

WHAT'S SAID WHEN YOU'RE NOT IN THE ROOM?

If you've looked after your brand that comment will be something positive: "You can depend on her", "He really thinks outside the box", "The customers love her", "He has fun and still gets the job done", "She'll go far in this business". Those are fantastic brand reputations to have.

Or maybe it will be a mix of the not so good and good: "He's a pushy guy but he gets things moving", "She looks like an airhead but she's sharp as a tack", "He comes across as a bit of an ogre but he's really loyal to his team". It's not quite as strong a brand message, but it's not so bad if the first bit is true and the second bit more than makes up for it.

What you don't want though is for it to be something entirely unflattering: "She never delivers", "It's all about him, never the team", "Everything she says is negative", "He's too much of a joker", "I'm surprised she's kept her job so long"...or worse.

Here's what I'm talking about...

Back in the days when I ran a press office, I was chatting to a journalist about an event I was holding. He asked who would be attending and as I mentioned each person's name he instantly added a comment. They were all complimentary apart from one. When I said the last name his response was, "That girl can drink!" The woman in question was renowned for going to events and getting so astonishingly drunk she would even forget where she lived. The fact she was also a great writer wasn't even mentioned – the negative aspect of her brand had overshadowed it.

Just think about the impact a negative comment could have on your business or your career – how just a few words could put the kibosh on you getting that million pound contract or that high profile promotion. Bad news has a habit of spreading further than good. You know yourself that when you're a satisfied customer, you might tell one or two people, but when you're dissatisfied, you'll tell as many people as you can (which can be thousands thanks to Facebook and Twitter). The same happens for your personal brand.

Here's what I'm talking about...

There's a CEO I know who, when he's going to be interviewing someone for a job, goes onto LinkedIn to see how they're connected. He then phones any contacts they have in common and asks the person what they think of the candidate. Their response – good and bad – goes a long way in helping him to make his decision to hire.

You can see why stress testing your perception of your brand is imperative; how else will you find out what people are saying about you? The bonus is, if there's anything untoward, you can tackle it.

| 1 | 2 | 3 | 4 | 5 |
GATHERING YOUR INGREDIENTS | DIGGING DEEPER | CHOOSING THE BEST BITS | YOUR REALITY CHECK | SETTING OUT YOUR RECIPE

This exercise is essentially about getting views on all the different aspects of your personal brand – otherwise known as 360° feedback. (For anyone who's not heard the term before, the 360° bit denotes the fact your insight into others' perceptions of you comes from all around.)

WHAT TO DO: Respondents

The first step is to come up with the list of people you want to ask for feedback. It's up to you how many respondents you include; a minimum of 10 is good because even if some people don't reply (and it's entirely likely that will happen) you should have enough responses to avoid feeling like Billy No-Mates. Conversely, a maximum of 20 is good because if everyone does reply (which happens on occasion) you can get confused by too much information.

Ideally, you want a mix of people to give you an all-round view: some you've known for years and some you've known only a short while (one client added his PA who'd only been working for him for three days). Try also to include internal people you've worked with or for, like your boss or reports, and some who are outside your business, like clients or suppliers. Even better, try to go for people you know will give you an honest answer and not just butter you up (another client included people they'd recently had a disagreement with).

Who you don't want are family or friends (one client snuck her mother-in-law onto the list, which made for interesting reading). We're talking about your personal brand in a business context and their views will be biased by knowing you out of work.

WHAT TO DO: Feedback channel

Once you have your list, of respondents you then have to decide how you want to ask them to give you the feedback. Your options are:

Option #1 – Email your respondents

Using email has a lot of benefits. Firstly, it gives you the chance to carefully word your questions to focus on areas you really want to know about. Secondly, it makes it easy for the person to respond, especially as they'll have time to think before typing their answers and can revisit and rewrite them as many times as they like before hitting the send button. And let's be honest, there's a third benefit: your email can be easily ignored if the person doesn't want to get involved.

On that note, there are lots of reasons why someone might choose not to give you feedback and it's important to remember that, contrary to your assumptions, most of them aren't about you. It might be their already busy workloads won't manage another task; they know they're not good with words so don't want to risk getting it wrong; they have a major issue in their life you're not aware of so your feedback isn't even making it onto their radar; they've given feedback in the past and it's been taken the wrong way so they've resolved never to do it again...the list goes on.

Yes, there's a chance their lack of response is because they don't like you or think you're rubbish and unworthy of their time, but if that's the case and you don't already know it, they were never going to be honest with you anyway.

Option #2 – Ask them on the phone or in person

For obvious reasons, this requires a bit more courage as you have to handle the situation if what's said isn't a bed of roses.

The upside is you can really dig down into people's answers by asking them to clarify something or ask an ad hoc question off the back of a response. However, you could also be lessening your respondents' level of comfort, which in turn could restrict the honesty of their answers.

Option #3 – Get someone else to ask for you

Using a go-between to act as a buffer between you and your respondents has a lot going for it: respondents have the confidence their answers will remain anonymous so can be more frank; reading all the feedback at once in a full report, rather than in dribs and drabs, means you get the whole picture and, along with that, some much needed perspective; and the go-between can add to that perspective by acting as a sounding board and saying where they interpreted answers differently from you.

Here's what I'm talking about...
I've delivered plenty of personal brand 360's and know first-hand how easy it is to misread what's been said. One client took a comment that he "only speaks to you if he needs to" as a criticism that he was distant, when in fact it was a compliment that he trusted the person to get on with their job.

It's a service I offer and one that many of my clients have said has been the pivotal point of them understanding their brand. (If you'd like to find out more about what's involved, get in touch.)

Option #4 – Use an existing tool

A quick search of the internet will bring up some online feedback tools, such as the one at www.reachcc.com/360v5register. They can be a great way of putting that buffer between you and your respondents without having to ask or pay someone to help. However, that added perspective will still be lacking and you won't be able to set the questions yourself, so might not get answers for the areas you really want to find out about.

WHAT TO DO: Questions

Once you've decided who you're asking and how you're asking them, you need to consider what you're asking them (unless you chose Option #4 in which case that's already decided). To give you the best chance of getting a reply it's best to limit yourself to no more than six or seven questions so you don't overwhelm the recipient.

Depending on which areas of your personal brand you want to focus on, you can compile your own questions or choose from the following, which are all open questions in that they require more than a 'yes' or 'no' answer:

Questions about your Image

Q: What stands out for you about my Image – how I look and sound?
Q: What clues did you pick up about me the first time we met?

Questions about your Skills/Strengths

Q: What would you consider to be my #1 Strength?
Q: What Skill do you consider me to be particularly good at?

Questions about your Behaviours

Q: What three words would you use to describe me?
Q: How would you describe my personality?

Questions about your Reputation

Q: What would you say I am known for?
Q: If someone mentioned my name, what comment would you add?

Questions about your Drivers*

Q: What do you think motivates me?
Q: When do you think I work at my best?

Questions about your Values*

Q: What would you say are my personal Values?

*As your Drivers and Values are deep-seated and very personal to you, it will be much more difficult for people to answer these questions, so think long and hard before including them.

Whichever questions you choose to ask though, there's one that you should always include:

Q: What could I do more or less of, or stop or start, to improve my personal brand?

The thought of asking "What's wrong with my brand?" (because that's pretty much what you're doing) will undoubtedly illicit a feeling of trepidation and possibly dread. But just like a Brazilian bikini-wax, any pain will be worth it. (I'm not speaking from experience here, I just figure no-one would be mad enough to have hot wax on their hoo-ha if there wasn't an upside!)

After all, it's much better to know if you're unwittingly damaging your brand than to blithely carry on being an eejit.

WHAT TO DO: Get on and ask

Once you've got your list of respondents, decided on your form of communication and drawn up your list of questions, all you have to do is ask for the feedback. There are a few things you should bear in mind when you do though:

- The most considerate way of asking for people's help is to give them a call and explain what you're doing. The personal touch is the least you can do in return for their time.

- If you'd rather send an email to your respondents, it's a good idea to write each one separately so you can personalise your message, again showing you value the person and their time.

- If you prefer to send a mass email, it's best to use the BCC (blind copy) option to keep the list of who you're asking confidential.

- Whether you're emailing or meeting in person, it's useful to set the scene for why you're requesting their help; you can mention it's part of working on your personal brand, which includes finding out how others see you as well as how you see yourself.

- Mention you value their opinion and hope they'll spare a short amount of time to give that to you. (If you can, it helps to include a guesstimate of how long it might take them.)

- Ask them to be as honest as possible and assure respondents their feedback will be taken with good humour and an open mind.

One last thing before you send your questions and answers start flooding in: remember the golden rule I shared with you on page 23:

Not everyone will buy your brand – accept it.

If you pay as much attention to the positive stuff as you do to any negative stuff, you just might find you enjoy the experience!

Here's what I'm talking about...
One client burst into tears when I delivered her feedback, saying "I finally realise, people see me as so much better than I see myself."

THE RESULTS ARE IN

You've got your feedback and have (hopefully) had a confidence boost from what people said because your view of your brand was close to that of your respondents. Don't expect a 100% match though – that's pretty much impossible – however, it can come pretty close.

Here's what I'm talking about...
One client was astounded at how accurate her respondents' feedback was and how quickly they'd picked up on her personal brand. Whilst she consciously toned down her personality, especially when meeting someone for the first time, it seems they were still getting the message loud and clear: she's self-assured, no-nonsense and business-like, with a softer side underneath. Knowing that gave her the confidence to simply be herself from the outset.

Even if your respondents didn't list the exact same ingredients you had, were their answers at least in the ballpark? Or were they so far off the field that you didn't even recognise yourself?

Experience has shown me that, for 95% of you, the feedback you've received will be pretty spot on; as one of my clients said, "Even the negative bits are things I already know about myself – I was just hoping people hadn't noticed!" That's good because you've stress tested your ingredients and they came up to scratch; it means that what you're already selling is pretty much what people are buying. But if you're like the 5% who have been surprised by what's been said, particularly if a fair few respondents said it, and particularly if it was less flattering than you'd expected, you need to take stock.

Firstly, have you read the feedback in the way it was intended? As I said on page 51, perspective can sometimes get warped. Putting a clear 24-hours between when you first get the response and re-reading it can often reveal a different interpretation.

Secondly, how many people gave that piece of feedback? If it was one person, you can chalk it up to a simple difference of opinion. If it was said by quite a number, it's worth taking heed.

If that's the case, why is there a discrepancy between your view of yourself and others'? Sometimes people have simply come at the questions from a different angle, leading to different answers. Sometimes though it's because some self-awareness has been lacking on your part and although it might hurt now, this new insight should be considered a gift; knowing what's wrong means you can set about putting it right. (Whereas if you continue to stick your fingers in your ears and sing "La la la – I can't hear you!" there's only one direction your personal brand will go...down.)

In that scenario you have two options: 1) make changes to your behaviour to address the mismatch of views (and if that's the case, you may want to get some professional help to form a plan of action). Or 2) accept 'it is what it is' and do your utmost to get more positive messages out there to counter the unfavourable ones (a case of framing the negative, which you'll read about on page 74).

NOW FOR THE FINAL RECIPE

Once you're happy with what you've learnt and are ready to crack on, carry on reading…

Now you have your feedback, take a minute to revisit your pared down list of ingredients and make any last changes based on your insight. (Other people can sometimes come up with ways of expressing your brand better than you can, so feel free to transfer any of their words to your list.) The final stage is to set about giving structure to your personal brand – the equivalent of writing the recipe for your signature dish using the pyramid I first set out on page 17 as your guide.

WHAT TO DO: Finding the themes

Get yourself a fresh sheet of paper and draw a line down the middle from top to bottom, splitting it in two vertically. Then draw two lines across the page at intervals a third and two thirds of the way down. You should now have a page split into six boxes, each of which you should head with one of the six brand elements:

VALUES	DRIVERS
REPUTATION	BEHAVIOURS
SKILLS/ STRENGTHS	IMAGE

Working through your final list of ingredients, transfer each one to your fresh page, writing it in the relevant box – or boxes if it's applicable to a couple of elements.

You might start seeing some themes emerge – connections between the ingredients that tie them together (like having the words 'ambitious', 'driven' and 'go-getter'). If that's the case, ask yourself if one of the words means more to you than another and consider choosing just for that one for your final recipe. Or think about whether there's an entirely different word that would encompass all three.

You may also start to see links forming between your ingredients, creating a sort of chain or process, like saying you 'think around corners' so 'spot the trends' and 'keep ahead of the game'. Or you 'ask the questions' to 'get to the nub of a problem' and 'stay focused on what needs to be done'. That's a good thing as you can pull them together in your pyramid.

Of course, you may end up completely stumped, in which case you might want to call in some help (you know where to find me).

Once you've created a bit of structure to your list, all that's required is to play around with the ingredients in each box to form a sentence or two for each layer of the pyramid. Remember – you don't have to use everything on there, a bit more paring can be a good thing.

I'm someone who always finds it easier to know what to do if I know what I'm aiming for, so here are some of my clients' pyramids (kept anonymous for confidentiality reasons) that I've helped to create. They're brief and to the point and while you can add more detail to yours, the aim is to have no more than two or three points in each of the six elements. That way your personal brand keeps its clarity, which in turn makes it easier for people to buy it.

I respect others and am always truthful –
I believe honesty can get you far.

I'm motivated by being my own person,
even if that's out of step with everyone else.

I'm known for delivering under pressure –
often with an 'added extra' that wasn't even asked for.

My personality is calm and composed
with an underlying drive and focus.

I enjoy solving problems and relish the challenge of
thinking differently to create an unexpected solution.

My creative thinking is reflected in my dress sense,
giving me a unique look that shows I like to be individual.

I always take responsibility – doing what I say I'll do – and operate in an
open way so people know where they stand and can be open in return.

I'm motivated by delivering change and feel proud when I've made
something happen where nobody else would or could.

I'm known for bringing projects back to life, because when I've
picked something up I don't put it down again until I've delivered
the results people need.

Determination is my middle name. I'm a positive, enthusiastic person
who enjoys working with positive, enthusiastic people.

I quickly assimilate new information and don't get phased by getting only
half the story, because I'll know where to go looking for the other half.

I take time over my appearance and look different from everyone else in a stylish,
co-ordinated way (I'm known for matching my colourful shoes and accessories).

I have a strong moral compass and my principles are to have empathy with others by being honest and down-to-earth.

I'm motivated by living life to the max with clear goals matched by a busy mind always looking for new challenges.

I'm known for using my creative thinking to be disruptive, always asking, "Why does it have to be?" in order to get the best for clients and staff.

My personality is positive, dynamic, genuine and fun, making me accessible to people at all levels.

I have a natural talent for communication and organisation – a combination which gives people the confidence to follow me. Plus my commercial awareness and financial background create a potent mix.

My style looks and sounds straightforward, though I listen more than talk because I'm genuinely interested in others.

I value fairness for others, particularly the vulnerable; they deserve a space to be brilliant.

I want to live my life helping lots of people to make lots of little changes that can create a big difference. Challenges are my drug.

I'm different from the charity norm – I think and act like an entrepreneur and won't put limits on myself, so achieve a lot.

My personality is led by my dogged determination. I take whatever is thrown at me, surfing the sea of uncertainty and calmly doing what's required.

I pick up information quickly then speedily think through the consequences. Once I have an idea I'll work out the shortest distance from A to B, thinking nothing of knocking on doors to get us there quicker.

I communicate an extrovert persona to ensure people feel at ease and have a good time though I'm a private person away from the limelight.

If you're positive, better things happen to you. The silver lining is always there if you look from a different perspective.

Starting from scratch floats my boat and I'm driven by putting in the hours and hitting deadlines because working hard is a sign that you care.

I'm known for starting from scratch and delivering things people said couldn't be done, which go on to become cornerstones of the business.

I have a drive and relentless pursuit to get things done and am a stickler for order because it's the little things that add to the efficiency.

I make it my job to understand what people bring to the table, then when the time's right I get them there, allocate responsibilites and give them the freedom to get on with the job.

I'm conservative and orderly in my appearance, reflecting the fact I stay calm and composed even when things go wrong.

I care about people and I care about the way we treat people. I'm transparent and trusting with the truth.

I'm committed to an optimal solution for everyone – the business, my team and me – because being respected matters to me.

I'm known for my commitment to doing better and delivering more, bringing the business context and people together.

I'm pragmatic and practical, keeping a sense of humour and a level head whatever the situation, because I always deliver.

My ability to read people means I know how to switch them on to what I'm saying so they know where they stand and trust me to lead us where we're headed.

My tailored style shows there's no faffing, just quiet confidence and polished delivery topped with a touch of something different.

THE FIRST STEP

Woo hoo! You have now created your very own, very fabulous, very personal brand. Get you! (If you haven't quite got there, creating brand pyramids is part of my service so drop me a line to find out more.)

If you're anything like me when I completed mine, you might be thinking, "So what the heck do I do with it now?" Some people I've worked with have chosen to carry it around with them and use it as a confidence boost in times of need – either focusing their mind before going into an important meeting or as a sense-check afterwards. Some have chosen to share it with their team so people can better understand and work with them. Others have pulled out aspects of their pyramid into different formats to help communicate their brand using consistent messages.

The second part of this book is devoted to **Promoting Your Personal Brand**, but even if you never get to that section, you'll have already gained something from the experience so far: confidence.

- The confidence that comes from understanding what makes you tick.
- The confidence that comes from defining who you are and what you have to offer.
- The confidence that comes from believing in that so you can just be yourself.
- The confidence that comes from understanding how others see you.
- The confidence that comes from accepting not everyone will buy your brand.
- The confidence that comes from shushing the voice in the back of your head saying, "What do they think of me?" and listening instead to the one saying, "What do I think of them?"

Here's what I'm talking about...

When I first met Sue, I instantly liked her: she was big and bold and ballsy. As she shared her story though, it seemed the Sue I was seeing was certainly not the Sue she showed other people. In fact, she said she went out of her way to be "what my boss wants me to be" and had suppressed the real Sue her whole career – over 25 years. That was starting to take its toll; she hated her job, had disengaged from her colleagues and was sinking into depression. As she told me this, her whole physiology changed: she drooped her shoulders, her voice went quiet and she just looked lost.

We continued chatting and she mentioned in passing that she'd written a screenplay. I was blown away by this and as she told me more – that it was a comedy, a little bit oddball, with a bit of bad language (mirroring her personality to a tee) – she became more animated, her shoulders lifted and she was beaming. When I asked what her colleagues thought about it, she replied, "I haven't told them." She thought it would be wholly unprofessional to do so and anyway, they wouldn't like her humour.

So we started working on her personal brand – the authentic one – and before we'd even got half way through, she changed. It was so dramatic a mutual acquaintance commented on it to me, saying Sue was like a new woman.

When I next met Sue she was radiant and told me she couldn't believe how much time she'd wasted being someone she wasn't. Now she was going to client meetings and when they said, "Did you have a good weekend?" she'd say, "Well I was working on my screenplay..." which, of course, would illicit further questions and allowed her to talk about her brand even more.

People got to see and hear the real Sue and because of that she found they were buying her brand more quickly. She also found she was enjoying her work again because she'd stopped stressing about being someone else and started promoting the fact she had a hell of a lot to offer just as she was.

12 months later I received an email from Sue talking about an event she'd attended. She said, "A year ago I would have struggled with how to respond to such a really diverse group of people, whereas this time I was just myself: sometimes my polite and gracious self, sometimes my humorous self. I had such a good time and am so happy being able to be the authentic 'me' in any company and any situation."

PART 2: PROMOTING YOUR PERSONAL BRAND

WHY IT'S OK TO BLOW YOUR OWN TRUMPET

Gaining confidence from your brand is one thing (and a very good thing at that) but if you really want to squeeze every last pip out of it, you need to go out there and share it with everyone else. It's time to promote your brand!

As I said at the beginning of this book, I come across many people who subscribe to the view that blowing your own trumpet 'just isn't done' and that doing a good job is all that's required to get ahead. Well maybe that was true 20 years ago, but if you take that tack today you'll get left behind like an odd sock in the laundrette of life.

With so many people, services and products to choose from, if you're not proving your worth, the assumption might be that you don't offer any real value. After all, you can be the hardest working person in your office – getting in earliest, leaving latest, not taking lunch, putting in all the hours – but if no-one knows you're the hardest working person in the office it won't make a jot of difference.

Promoting your personal brand is vital.

EGO NO-GO

If your first reaction to that is a fear that you could be seen as an arrogant egomaniac, I have some reassuring news: the fact you are worried at all means you have an inbuilt safety-valve that will stop it happening. (Think of it as a switch that will short circuit if you get too big for your boots.) It's the people who don't worry about sounding arrogant who are the ones with zero self-awareness and absolutely no idea they're acting like complete prats.

Here's what I'm talking about...

In his book, *An Astronaut's Guide to Life On Earth*, Commander Chris Hadfield (the guy whose rendition of David Bowie's *Space Oddity*, sung on the International Space Station, received millions of views on YouTube) gives some great advice for making the right impression. He says, *"In any new situation, whether it involves an elevator or a rocket ship, you will almost certainly be viewed one of three ways. As a minus one: actively harmful, someone who creates problems. Or as a zero: your impact is neutral and doesn't tip the balance one way or another. Or you'll be seen as a plus one: someone who actively adds value.*

"Everyone wants to be a plus one, of course. But proclaiming your plus one-ness at the outset almost guarantees you'll be perceived as a minus one, regardless of the skills you bring to the table or how you actually perform. This might seem self-evident but it can't be because so many people do it."

In actual fact, instead of trumpeting your brand like a latter day Louis Armstrong, what you need to be doing is leveraging a skill we Brits have in spades...subtlety. Start off aiming to be a zero, making understated toots instead of a thunderous fanfare, and people will soon realise for themselves you're a plus one.

GIVE US A CLUE

It's all about those little clues I talked about on page 22. People are picking up information about you all the time, so look at each and every clue as an opportunity to deliver a message about your brand. Because if every time someone comes into contact with you – whether in person, on the phone or online – they get a nugget of information with a consistent, clear message, they can start to piece it all together into a bigger picture of what and who they're buying.

They'll be using their reference library plus a whole heap of assumptions to decipher those clues. So it's a good idea to work out in advance what you'd like them to think and how you might get that across. For instance, mentioning in your online profile that you recently swam The Channel gives clues that you're physically fit, determined, goal-focused and mentally strong. Alternatively, saying you run a donkey sanctuary in your spare time suggests you're charitable, caring and focused on those who can't help themselves. Or seeing you dressed in vintage clothes could give pointers to the fact you're an individualist who's happy in their own skin, has a creative flair and appreciates the quality of a bygone age.

However, other clues you give might fall into a grey area: things to do with your religious beliefs, political leanings, sexual preferences or anything else that can cause a strong moral reaction. That's when it's important to have a clear idea about how much of your brand you want to reveal, which is a dilemma that faces us all. Being authentic must remain a cornerstone of any personal brand but sometimes who we are includes things that may cause offence to others – or at least make them think we're not their cup of cha.

SET YOUR RUNG ON THE LADDER

So how do you walk the line between being authentic and still getting the buy-in of your audiences? The answer is to work it out in advance so you have a clear idea of where your brand should and shouldn't wander.

Step 1 – Set the guidelines

Imagine a ladder, where the top rung is you at your most professional (suited and booted and only talking business) and the bottom rung is you at your most relaxed (out with your mates and not worrying if 'just the one' turns into two, three or four).

Keep moving down from the top rung until you find one where it feels comfortable for you to pitch your personal brand. (Whatever you do, don't stay at the top – the whole point of personal branding is to make it personal.) Decide what sits 'above the line' that's perfectly acceptable to share and what sits 'below the line' that you're going to keep private…then stick to it.

Step 2 – Don't hide who you are

If there's an aspect of your personal brand that has the potential to put people off, the temptation is to keep it below the line. But if you know your faith/politics/sexuality is something that, if taken away, would undermine your whole being, be true to yourself and keep it in. Changing your behaviour to the point that you stop being you is the quickest way for people to stop buying your brand; they can smell a fraud at 20 paces and it's an aroma that says you can't be trusted.

Step 3 – Get the balance right

None of this is to say you should ignore others' views (you're not a Cabinet Minister), but instead of stopping your behaviour completely, simply tone it down. Taking the example of religion, I read a LinkedIn profile once of a man who mentioned, as part of explaining something else, that he was a Christian. That alone was enough to make me buy his personal brand – not for religious reasons (theology isn't my thing) but because he had the courage of his convictions and that told me he was being authentic.

The upshot is to have faith in your personal brand: if you're a morris-dancing pagan who's a paid-up member of the Green Party and spend your spare time collecting antique clocks with your civil partner, don't be afraid to let people know (you'd certainly be memorable). Accept that, while some people are going to buy into you big time, others won't like what you have to offer...but they're probably not the people you want to be working alongside anyway.

Here's what I'm talking about...

When Mary and I started working on her brand, she used phrases like "seeking a greater purpose" and "believing in a higher power" to describe her Drivers. Those convictions have made Mary the woman she is, but she felt that any reference to 'spirituality' in her brand might turn people off. We decided that excluding them meant she wasn't being authentic, so instead we dialled them down using more subtle phrases. Her biography now reads: 'Growing up on a farm, Mary learnt a reverence and respect for Mother Nature that gave her a deep appreciation for living a purposeful life.'

RELATIONSHIP HOOKS

The real beauty of giving people clues like the fact you swam The Channel, run a donkey sanctuary or collect antique clocks is that they offer an added bonus: a 'relationship hook'. Revealing something personal gives people a hook to grab onto that will steer the conversation away from just business and into something more individual. (And of course you'll be looking out for their relationship hooks in order to do the same.) Focusing on the person, not just their job title, means you can build your relationship much quicker than if you simply talked shop – and when people are buying people that matters.

Here's what I'm talking about...

I was meeting an MD for the first time who, as part of welcoming me, asked if I'd travelled far. "Skipton," I replied. "I don't know the place," he said, so I enlightened him by describing the view from my office. "I look onto a field full of sheep and cows, then I've got my chickens in the front garden and my bees in the back." "You keep chickens...so do I!" he replied. What followed was a 10 minute discussion about our hens, followed by another 10 minutes about bees and a further 10 about pigs (he kept those too). Half an hour later we got round to business and after a brief discussion he said, "Great...let's get started." It wasn't my pitch that convinced him I was the woman for the job. It was the fact I'd offered a relationship hook and he'd taken it, forming his perceptions of me along with them. (The reference library in his head interpreted keeping chickens as a good thing.) If I'd answered his original question with the usual business small-talk though, things could have been very different.

SAME CLUE, DIFFERENT MESSAGE

There is a caveat to add about giving clues to your brand. In the words of Huey Lewis, *"The power of love is a curious thing: make one man weep, make another man sing."* (Too true Huey, too true.)

It's a fact of life that one person's perception of your personal brand will differ from another's, because the myriad of things that have come together to form their reference library will dictate how they'll decipher the clues to your brand. Here are some examples to explain:

What do you think when you see a messy desk? Some see it as a sign of creativity, that the person is too busy coming up with ideas to bother with the small stuff – like filing. Others (and as an occasional neat-freak I'd include me in this) see it as a sign of disorder, that the person isn't on top of things and can't work effectively. One is a positive reading of the clue, the other is a negative one.

And what do you think when you hear someone's ringtone and it's the theme from *The Archers*? That they have traditional values and are an upstanding member of society (after all, the storylines are a far cry from the drama of *Eastenders*). Or do you think they're outdated and likely to be a stick-in-the-mud fuddy duddy? Both views are legitimate.

Or during the Christmas season when colleagues start to adorn themselves with yuletide accessories (think tinsel earrings, Santa ties and badges of Rudolph with a flashing nose) what clues do they give? Do you read them as, "This person's obviously a lot of fun and enjoys themself," or as, "That's totally unprofessional and they should spend more time on their work and less on mucking around." (Or what I think, which is, "Please don't let me get stuck in a lift with them!")

Every clue people get about your personal brand can be taken different ways, but if you haven't thought what those clues are and what you want them to say, you've even less chance that people's perceptions will be accurate. The moral is: so long as you've thought about what you want to say and, in your mind, your clues are saying it, that's all there is to it. People with similar brands will be on your wavelength, view your clues in the same way and buy into your brand. And people who view them differently might not buy into your brand at all (even Huey's power of love can't change that) but if you're so different anyway, that may not be a bad thing.

Here's what I'm talking about...

What would you think if we were arranging a date for a meeting and I pulled out my Filofax? Would you, like one client, say it fitted me to a tee because it was different from the norm and had a retro feel (which I'd say matched my brand). Or would you, as someone else was, be surprised I had one as you viewed it as old-fashioned and backwards (which I'd like to think I'm not). Neither was right nor wrong, they were just saying how they saw it...although I'm obviously on the same wavelength as the first person.

SETTING YOUR BRANDWIDTH

We've talked about setting limits when it comes to what you will and won't reveal about your brand, but to cover all the elements of your pyramid you need to build a bigger picture: your brandwidth.

Like the bandwidth of a radio station, your personal brand has a range within which you can dial up or dial down your Image, Skills, Behaviours, etc and still send out a strong signal that's 100% genuine. But just like a radio station, if you go too far outside that range, all others will get from you is static.

Some people have a wide brandwidth; their character is naturally flexible so they can adapt to match the people around them and still do it in an authentic way. Others have a brandwidth that's much narrower; their character is more defined as 'what you see is what you get' so there's a lot less variation. This diagram shows you what I mean:

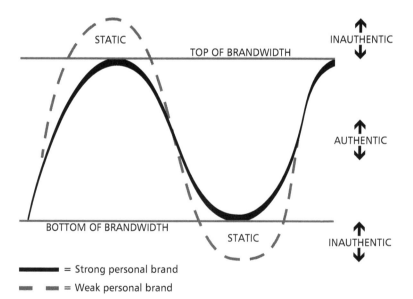

The top of your brandwidth is you at your most professional, where you dial up to for those important occasions like an interview or delivering a presentation. Image-wise you wear the smartest version of your style (which doesn't automatically mean a suit, because that may not be what you're all about). You talk more eloquently (the equivalent of putting on your telephone voice). Your personality is more pronounced (delivered with more energy). And your behaviour is more polished (what you might call the 'grown up' version of you).

The bottom of your brandwidth is a more casual version of you (but still professional). It's the level you dial down to when you're meeting people who are also likely to have dialled down, for instance on a team building day or at an informal dinner with a long-standing client. Your image will be more casual (which doesn't necessarily equate to wearing jeans), your conversation more chatty (with more colloquial language and perhaps the odd swear word) and your behaviour more relaxed (not quite 'out with your mates' but in the ballpark).

It's important to decide where your parameters lie, because if you go outside your brandwidth and change your behaviour too far from the norm, people will quickly spot you're a fraud. As Oscar Wilde said, "Be yourself. Everyone else is taken."

Here's what I'm talking about...

A woman on one of my workshops admitted she changed her brand quite markedly to match who she was with. She told us how she'd visited a client in The City one morning, so wore a conservative suit. Then she'd gone home and changed into an entirely different outfit that was more casual and quirky, before visiting another client who owned an art gallery. When quizzed, she realised the real her sat somewhere in the middle of the spectrum and if she ever bumped into either client when she was 'herself', she'd be rumbled. The easier and more honest option was to vary her image within her brandwidth.

FRAMING THE NEGATIVE

Whilst it's healthy to accept that not everyone will read your personal brand clues as you mean them, there are times when a negative view could be affecting your brand and a bit more direction is called for.

Let's take the example of accents – something that can conjure up a whole host of preconceived ideas in people's heads. A study by the Aziz Corporation found that people with a Home Counties accent were considered by 77% of those surveyed to be generally successful in business, whereas 64% regarded those with a Liverpudlian tone as being generally unsuccessful. So if you have a strong Scouse accent the assumption might be that you're lacking in the intelligence department – in which case, preventative measures should be taken.

Here's what I'm talking about...
Kate is a director who has a broad Yorkshire accent (although she stops short of saying "Ee bah gum"). She was concerned about how she came across when she spoke because people often hear her voice and assume she's not too bright. We discussed how she could counteract that and one tactic she now uses is to say, "As y'can hear I'm a Yorkshire lass and I'm a lot smarter than I sound!" all with a twinkle in her eye and a grin on her face. Not only does it show she's aware of how she sounds, it reveals her sense of humour too.

Another thing that can work against you is being young (or just looking younger than your years) and therefore automatically considered inexperienced. Or the flipside of that, which is being seen as over-the-hill. Having a physical disability could make people think you're incapable. Or having a previous employer with a bad reputation might lead to you being tarred with the same brush. If you happen to have something about your brand that could be misconstrued, you could do well to take action and flag it up.

In fact, my friend Ashley Boroda who used to work with stand-up comedians told me how, if a person had a distinctive feature, such as big ears, they'd make sure the first joke told was about that; it let the audience know the comedian knew what they were thinking and put them at ease so they weren't distracted for the rest of the set. I'm not saying you need to make fun of yourself, but I am saying it's good to be up front if something is obvious.

To frame a negative you need to pinpoint the upside of the situation (and there will always be one). To do that, think about the benefits that come with your particular elephant in the room and find ways to introduce them into the conversation so you create a positive perception before the negative one can take hold.

For example, smoking is something many people see in a negative light, to the extent that it can be a deal-breaker for them buying someone's brand. However, there are positive aspects to smoking and some I've been told by my clients are: being in the smokers' huddle means you pick up all sorts of titbits about what's going that you wouldn't otherwise; you form strong relationships with other smokers that can help get business done; and you can do some of your best thinking with a cigarette in your hand. That's what needs to be talked about to offset all the bad stuff.

Sometimes though, being seen in a negative light isn't just down to you, in which case a more stringent plan of action may be needed.

Here's what I'm talking about...

A woman approached me after one of my presentations asking for advice on handling a work situation where her new boss was saying negative and derogatory things behind her back. (She knew this because her team had brought it to her attention.) She'd already tackled her boss to insist he stop, but had got the same response as if she'd talked to a brick wall. She'd also tried taking the matter up with her boss's boss, who had listened but passed no comment and taken no action. She was at a loss what to do, highly stressed and fearing that, if her boss kept broadcasting his lies to all and sundry, her reputation would be in the doghouse. However, while it's true your brand is what people say about you when you're not in the room, it doesn't carry much weight if the person saying it is a complete twonk.

Although someone with a strong, credible reputation will be perceived as having strong, credible views, someone whose reputation is weak and unreliable will be seen to have views to match. The fact this woman's team were the ones who told her what was going on showed they had already discounted what the boss said. And the fact her boss's boss chose not to comment may signal she's acutely aware of this man's rap sheet (she certainly didn't stick up for his actions). Which doesn't make what he was doing right, but it does take some sting out of the tail.

My advice for anyone in this situation is to follow what the celebrities (or at least their PR agencies) do when scandal hits: generate loads of positive press to counter the bad stuff and push the alleged skeletons as far back into the closet as possible – or at least off the first page of Google searches.

That means being seen doing the right things by the right people, putting across positive messages about your brand, enlisting the help of others to correct any misconceptions and hoping that eventually the person creating the bad press will give up and quit bitching. What you definitely shouldn't do is bury your head in the sand and do nothing.

A final note of caution: just because you assume an aspect of your brand is being perceived negatively, it may not be, so only take action if you're sure the person in front of you is forming the wrong opinion. Otherwise you could be drawing attention to something that wasn't a problem in the first place!

EVERY CLUE IS AN OPPORTUNITY

Now we've set some ground rules for 'how' you go about promoting your personal brand, it's time to talk about 'where' you promote it. However, you need to understand that promoting your brand isn't a one-off gig. Just like any other brand, you need to keep repeating your message for it to really sink in. (Nike hasn't changed its *Just Do It* strapline in over 25 years.) Your personal brand works much the same way: you need to keep up a steady stream of impressions to really get buy-in. That's a lot easier than you might think because, if you're canny, you'll be channelling positive messages about your brand via every conceivable way that people come into contact with you...and I mean every!

Sometimes people pick up clues to your brand via written channels:

- They note the language in your email
- They spot the info in your email signature
- They Google your name and see the results
- They read your website biography
- They view your LinkedIn profile
- They catch your LinkedIn updates
- They read your blog
- They peruse your Twitter profile
- They monitor your Tweets
- They browse your Facebook updates
- They receive your out of office message
- They read a report or memo you've written
- They see your job title on your business card
- They check out your slides while you deliver your presentation
- They analyse your CV
- They read the covering letter
- They get a note from you and spot your handwriting
- They see your signature
- They decipher your text message

Sometimes they pick up clues via auditory channels:

- They speak to you on the phone
- They get your voicemail message
- They ask, "Hi how are you?" and listen to your reply
- They overhear you talking to someone else
- They overhear others talking about you
- They listen to a presentation you're giving
- They take part in a conference call with you
- They Skype you
- They meet with you either one-to-one or in a larger group
- They ask, "What do you do?" and listen to your 'elevator pitch'
- They hear the ringtone on your mobile
- They pick up on your accent
- They gauge your voice's tone, speed and strength
- They notice how much you talk versus how much you listen

They might also pick up clues via physical channels:

- They clock the car you drive up in (or the motorbike or bicycle you ride) plus the state it's in
- They note your timekeeping: turning up for meetings, responding to messages, meeting deadlines
- They check out the clothes and shoes you're wearing
- They assess your hairstyle and make-up
- They scrutinise your accessories: your watch, cufflinks, jewellery (including wedding ring), bag, pen, pad, mobile phone, mobile phone cover
- They spot the make and model of your technology
- They judge your levels of physical fitness and hygiene
- They feel the pressure of your handshake
- They interpret your eye contact and body language
- They measure the personal space you give
- They see you deliver a presentation
- They handle your business card

- They survey the state of your desk
- They observe your photos and mementos
- They notice the pen you use
- They look at your LinkedIn, Twitter and Facebook photos
- They spot what's in the background when you Skype
- They catch a glimpse of your screen saver

That's a lot of things, isn't it? And it's not even an exhaustive list. You'll probably even recognise one or two that are your particular favourites for working people out but everyone's preference will be different. While you might think it's a bit over the top to have to give a consistent brand message through all of those channels, that's exactly what you need to do, because you have no way of knowing which of them will be having the impact.

GET THE AUDITORS IN

Before we crack on with the next section on how to get your brand out there, it's worth doing a quick audit of how you're currently faring. That way you can identify where you really need to up your game.

WHAT TO DO: On or off brand?

Go back through the lists you've just read – the written, auditory and physical channels – with your personal brand pyramid fixed firmly in your mind. For each one ask yourself:

Are the clues I give on brand, off brand or brand neutral?

When you're on brand, you'll look at the item in the list and think, "There's no doubting it, my brand comes across loud and clear (and positive) via that channel." When you're off brand, you'll look at the item and think, "I always feel uncomfortable with that and know I don't come across well."

When you're brand neutral, you'll look at the item and think, "It's not good and it's not bad but it could be better."

Make a note of the ones you think need some work so you can pay specific attention as you read on. Even better, ask someone else for their opinion – I'm always quick to give it when I do people's audits. You may think you have something sussed but find out you're wrong (as many of my clients have discovered!)

Remember that each of those examples is opportunity knocking; it's a channel through which you can send conscious yet subtle messages that show you, and your brand, in a positive light. To help you do that, the following three sections set out key areas where you should be tooting your horn – in the office, out and about and online – and each includes a host of simple, practical advice to show you how.

A final word on blowing your own trumpet: remember that not all advertising is good advertising, so think through the implications of every clue you put out there.

Here's what I'm talking about...

Whilst reading *The Metro* one morning, my eye was caught by a headline: *I've Passed With Horn-Ors*. It was about a young lady (I use the term loosely) called Elina who had recently been crowned Britian's Most Promiscuous Student after sleeping with three men a week during her time at Exeter University. Whilst my jaw was on the floor throughout the entire article, the bit that really made me shudder was Elina's closing comment: "I hope employers see it as a bit of fun and it shows I'm more confident than your average girl." Having spent 15 years of my career in PR where I learnt to put a positive spin on the direst news, even I felt it was pushing the envelope to believe this was a career enhancing, rather than career limiting, move. (Unless of course her future job prospects involve a pole and some platform stilettos.)

PROMOTING YOUR BRAND: IN THE OFFICE

If you're in business, I'm going to assume you spend a lot of time in the office, so that's where we'll begin promoting your brand. As the following sections show, the office offers a plethora of channels to start tooting your horn day-to-day.

LANGUAGE

I've chosen to start with a note about language because it's pertinent wherever you are – when you're out and about and online too (you'll find those sections later in the book). That's because language is the bread and butter of promoting your brand, so if you can get that bit right you'll already be a long way down the road.

ACCENTUATE THE POSITIVE

In this life there are two types of people: the 'can do' and the 'can't do'. Time spent with a 'can do' is like drinking half a dozen espressos on the trot – you come away fired up and full of enthusiasm. Being with a 'can't do' is like spending a bank holiday weekend in a caravan with the rain lashing at the windows and only a 100 piece jigsaw of a kitten to keep you company.

When it comes to your brand, being a 'can do' should be a no-brainer because it all boils down to one simple equation:

**Projection of a positive brand =
Perception of a positive brand =
Buy-in to your brand**

A big part of that projection is the language you use.

Here's what I'm talking about...
I was once at a conference where ex-Tory MP Virginia Bottomley was a speaker. She told a story about the time she had been Minister for the Environment but a cabinet reshuffle resulted in her being told she would become Minister for Health – to which she'd replied, "But I don't know anything about health." Her male colleague who was also getting a new position for which he had no experience simply said, "I'll bring a fresh pair of eyes to the subject." Spot the difference?

Here are some examples of 'can do' and 'can't do' language:

CAN'T DO: I can't get it finished today.
CAN DO: I can finish it tomorrow.

CAN'T DO: I'm sorry to bother you.
CAN DO: I appreciate your time on this.

CAN'T DO: Please do not hesitate to contact me with any queries.
CAN DO: Let me know if you have any questions.

CAN'T DO: It's good but it's not good enough.
CAN DO: It's good and it could be even better.

The meanings are the same but the 'can do' people are subtly projecting a positive personal brand. As you've seen, it goes further than 'can' and 'can't'. For instance, when you're asked to do something do you say, "No problem"? If so, you're subconsciously projecting a negative brand because the word the brain will hear is 'problem'. Instead, you could say, "I'd be happy to do that." The key word is 'happy' and that's much more positive. Or if you call someone and say, "Hi, it's only me," you're conveying a feeling of disappointment with the word 'only' that's entirely unnecessary. Here are some other words to think about:

Positive language

- I appreciate...
- I can...
- I'd be pleased to...
- I look forward to...
- If you can...
- May I suggest...
- I can help you...
- I'm grateful for...
- I'm happy to say that...
- I'd love the chance to...
- It's great that...
- I'm able to...
- The good thing is...
- You've made my day...
- You've really helped me...
- I'd value your...
- I'm glad you...
- Feel free to...
- You've done well to...
- Thank you.

Negative language

- I will not...
- I can't...
- I won't...
- I don't...
- I shouldn't...
- I'm unable to...
- I'm sorry but...
- I hate...
- I'm frustrated by...
- I'm afraid to say...
- I know you're busy but...
- I fail to understand...
- I insist...
- You didn't...
- No doubt you...
- You failed to...

When you're next typing an email or talking on the phone, think about what you're saying because it's a great opportunity for you to accentuate the positive and, along with it, your personal brand.

However, it's not only your words that need to be positive – your delivery of them does too. When a 'can do' person says, "I'm great at working with a team," the energy in their voice and the smile on their face makes sure you absolutely believe them. But if a 'can't do' person says the same thing, with a voice as flat as a pancake and a face as long as a gas man's mac, they'll never be believed.

7 WAYS TO SAY "NO"

There are, of course, times when it's impossible to avoid being a 'can't do' and saying "No" is what's required. However, even that can be tricky because, let's be honest, we're British and the direct approach isn't exactly in our DNA.

Saying "No" is something I often struggle with (although my ex-boss might disagree) but one day I came across a little gem of a blog by Celestine Chua on www.zenhabits.net that offered exactly the practical advice I needed.

So to help you keep your personal brand on the straight and narrow, here are her ways to say No/Nein/Niet/Non/Bugger off:

#1 – "I can't commit to this as I have other priorities at the moment."

This lets the person know your plate is full so they should hold off on this as well as future requests. You may also want to share what you're working on so the person can better understand your reply.

#2 – "Now's not a good time as I'm in the middle of something. How about we reconnect at X time?"

This method is a great way to (temporarily) hold off the request and by suggesting another time the person doesn't feel completely blown off.

#3 – "I'd love to do this but…"

It's a gentle way of breaking "No" to the other party. It's encouraging as it lets the person know you like the idea (of course, only say this if you do like it).

#4 – "Let me think about it first and I'll get back to you."

This is more like a "Maybe" than a straight out "No" – though if you're uninterested don't lead them on.

#5 – "This doesn't meet my needs now but I'll be sure to keep you in mind."

This helps the person know there's nothing wrong with what they're offering and at the same time, by saying you'll keep them in mind, it signals you are open to future opportunities.

#6 – "I'm not the best person to help on this. Why don't you try X?"

If you're being asked for help in something which you a) can't contribute much to and b) don't have resources to help, let them know they're looking at the wrong person. If possible, turn your rejection into a positive by referring them to someone they can follow-up with so they don't face a dead end.

#7 – "No, I can't."

The simplest and most direct way to say it. We build up too many barriers in our mind to saying "No" so don't think about it and just say it outright. You'll be surprised when the reception isn't half as bad as you imagined it to be.

> ### Here's what I'm talking about...
> I've used #7 on occasion, usually when approached with a business proposition that's not a great fit for my business. I put a British spin on it though and say, "Thank you, though I'd rather not." It works a treat.

If all else fails and you just can't bring yourself to say the word, you can always feign illness and do a runner instead.

MAKE IT ENGAGING

Being positive is just for starters – it should be the minimum you're doing. If you really want to get payback for your brand, you have to go a bit further to stand out from the crowd. You may think, "Well, if I'm promoting my brand in the first place I'll already be standing out," but that's not a given. You could be sending out all the messages in the world about who you are and what you have to offer, but if you're using the wrong language you could become just another 'me too'.

Me toos talk in bland jargon, sticking to the tried and tested business-speak of the corporate world where they "manage operational change" or "facilitate organisational transformation". It's the equivalent of seeing 10mph signs everywhere.

Here's what I'm talking about...
I once read a newspaper story about a building site where signs for a 9½mph speed limit had been put up. This was obviously barmy especially when, as one builder pointed out, most site vehicles don't have a speedometer. However, the site foreman explained that when they'd had 10mph signs, no-one had taken any notice – they'd become like wallpaper. But since putting up the new signs the speeds (and number of accidents) had dropped. That's because making people's brains go "Whoa boy! Wasn't expecting that!" meant they switched on and paid attention – which is exactly what you want people to do when they come across your brand.

The trouble with communicating in 10mph language is people stop listening and you cease to be memorable. And if people don't remember you, how will they consider you for that promotion you've been longing for, or that new job offer that would earn you the big bucks, or that contract that would take your business to another level?

You need to deliver more of your messages at 9½mph, using phrases that go zing in people's synapses and lodge there like a piece of spinach in your teeth. A good way to find alternatives is to call on Mr Roget and his *Thesaurus* again. Instead of just saying you're 'approachable' how about saying you're 'cordial', 'courteous', 'big-hearted' or 'gallant'? (When was the last time you heard that?) Or instead of saying you're 'creative' how about saying you're 'visionary', 'inventive', 'original' or 'imaginative'? And instead of saying you're 'effective' how about saying you're 'artful', 'deft', 'adroit' or 'expert'? They're certainly not 10mph!

Better still, try and think of a metaphor for what you're saying that will really bring your brand to life in people's minds. A woman in one of my workshops once said, "So instead of saying I'm energetic I should say I'm like Tigger." Exactly – I mean...you wouldn't forget her in a hurry!

MIND YOUR LANGUAGE

You can't have a section on language without covering the subject of swearing ("Oh yes you bloody well can!") While the rules surrounding manners are pretty black and white – picking your nose in public or pushing in front of old ladies in the bus queue are still frowned on – when it comes to swearing its increasing prominence in daily life means things become a little more grey.

If, like me, you're prone to using colourful language as part of your normal conversation (not the full lexicon of profanities but certainly more than "flip" and "fudge") it's worth considering what it's doing to your personal brand.

On one hand you need to take into account that some people find swearing of any ilk offensive and that's going to affect how they buy your brand. On the other hand, you need to be authentic and if the odd swear word is part of who you are, to stop it completely might be outside your brandwidth…a huge no-no. My advice is to aim for the middle ground, using the swear words that even your granny might use rather than the stronger ones that cross further over the line. It's letting people know in a relatively gentle way that swearing is part of your personal brand and if they're offended by that, you're probably not going to get along anyway, so better to know now than to find out later. However, there will be people who hear you swear and it makes them think "They're just like me"– the upshot of which is you've speeded up the process of them buying into you.

> ### Here's what I'm talking about…
> I'd delivered a seminar to a group of senior executives and said the phrase "no shit Sherlock" mid-way through to emphasise a point. Afterwards, one pinstriped delegate commented, "I like a woman who talks like a man." (He meant the fact I'd said "shit" and not the gruffness of my voice!) He'd bought into my brand precisely for my swearing.

As with any part of your brand, take notice of your brandwidth and dial your swearing up and down depending on the audience – and if you're not sure, ask the person you're with how they feel about it. I often do and 99% say it's not a problem because they're relieved they can swear too. (When I asked one client if she was OK with swearing her answer was, "F*** yes!")

Some Dos and Don'ts about Language
- **DO** use positive language – it creates a positive perception of your brand.
- **DON'T** be afraid of saying "No".
- **DON'T** use 10mph language – it becomes wallpaper.
- **DO** use a *Thesaurus* to find words that go at 9½mph.
- **DO** adjust your swearing to better suit your audience but **DON'T** stop it completely if that's not authentically you.

IMAGE

Out of all the things that make up a personal brand, Image can have the most instant impact, because it's the 'packaging' that gives clues to what's on offer. Think about it: if you're in a room of people and you spot someone walking in, within one-tenth of a second you've formed an opinion about them. They might not have even opened their mouth or shaken your hand, but you already have a pretty good idea whether you're buying their brand.

What's influencing that opinion? Everything, from how they look (their physique, body language, eye contact, hairstyle, make-up, clothing, accessories, personal hygiene) to how they sound (their accent, tone, volume, language)…it's all adding to the picture.

ADDRESSING YOUR DRESSING

Ask yourself: "What do I want my Image to tell people about me?" The answer to that should reflect your personal brand.

Here's what I'm talking about...
A former-client of mine, Deri, is in his 30s and always wears a three-piece pinstripe suit, even though the style is associated with people much older than him. He does it to reflect his old-fashioned values, which form the foundation of his brand, and also because he wants to let people know he's no ordinary guy (there aren't too many others his age sporting a waistcoat and a pocket handkerchief).

When you're deciding what to wear in the morning, take time to think about what your key brand attributes are and whether your Image conveys them…in all its forms. (We all know someone whose attempt to convey a smart brand was let down by the fact their shirt collar was threadbare, or their pinstripe suit and snazzy tie were contradicted by a mouth full of yellowing teeth and nicotine breath.) After all, if you look the part, you'll feel the part.

Here's what I'm talking about...
Research by Adam Galinsky and Hajo Adam at Columbia University has shown there's a direct link between what you wear and how your brain thinks. They called the phenomenon 'enclothed cognition' and the nuts and bolts of the study are that the state of our bodies affects our thoughts and our clothing plays a huge part in that state – especially if it has symbolic meaning. They asked people to do a series of mental tasks either wearing a white lab coat (something associated with scientists, intellect and analysis) or simply wearing their own clothes. Those who wore the coat found their brain registered the 'enclothed cognition' that made them think they were clever old egg-heads, leading them to make half as many errors as those who didn't wear the coat. Interestingly, when those wearing the coat were told it wasn't a scientist's lab coat but actually a painter's overcoat, their rates of accuracy went down; the symbolic meaning had gone and the brain reacted accordingly.

If you have clothes that give you enclothed cognition in a positive way, put your best brand foot forward by making sure you wear them (appreciating of course that not many of us could pull off a white lab coat without looking a complete numpty).

Wear those pinstripes that imbue tradition (and bolster your conventional approach) or those high heels that radiate authority (and make you feel like a powerhouse). Wear that fluorescent tie that loves to get noticed (feeding your exhibitionist streak) or that hand-crafted necklace that's one-of-a-kind (and makes you feel unique). Wear that fluffy cardigan that's soft and warm (and seems like it's giving you a hug) or that sports watch (delivering its messages of health and fitness). You'll soon find the attributes you're experiencing are the ones you're projecting.

However, while dressing at the top of your brandwidth can be relatively stress-free, dressing down can be an entirely different kettle of fish.

DRESSING DOWN OR DRESSING GOWN?

Dress Down Day. Three words that strike fear into many an office worker's heart because, while knowing how to look smart comes easily to most, 'business casual' is a lot harder. Unless your firm has a permanent dress-down policy, knowing what to wear in these instances can be a bit of a minefield – especially if you want to keep giving consistent messages about your brand.

It's just as bad when the sunny weather hits and dressing for business sometimes gets confused with dressing for the beach. But remember…people are gathering clues to your brand all the time so it's good to question the impact they're having:

- Wearing a T-shirt with the name of a band on it is fine, but if you're old enough to be their father how hip can you be?
- Your tattoo may be a work of art, but does a butterfly perched on a rainbow deliver the gravitas you need?
- Flip flops might be comfortable, but will your weird little toe that's longer than the rest of them really put your best foot forward?
- Hairy armpits might be Mother Nature's way of delivering pheromones to attract a mate, but did she ever have to sit opposite when you put your hands behind your head?
- A shorter skirt might aid the circulation of air around your hoo-ha, but do you want people to think that after work you'll be going to your part-time job as a hooker?
- White trousers might be on trend, but what clues will people get from the natty G-string that's showing through?

The bottom line: there's a balance between dressing down and losing your credibility, so take the time to get it right. If your team sees you in a sharp, pinstriped suit one day then cargo shorts and sandals the next, the contrast sends conflicting messages and makes them question who the real you is.

To keep things aligned, it's important to set your own dress code by using your brandwidth to establish clear boundaries of what 'dressed up' and 'dressed down' look like. Then stick to it...even if it's at odds with everyone else. (I once read a tweet about a guy who wore a tuxedo on his company's Dress Down Day because looking casual just wasn't him – respect!)

Here's what I'm talking about...

I was once met in reception by a client who was dressed in a non-descript, oversized rugby shirt and baggy chinos, neither of which flattered his larger physique. During the session that followed, I asked him which clothes he felt represented his brand. He replied, "A Hugo Boss shirt, no tie, and smart trousers." I then asked him whether his current outfit reflected his brand, to which the answer was, "No, but it's Dress Down Friday so you have to." That wasn't actually true. He'd let corporate culture dictate his attire and it was doing nothing to promote his brand – or boost his confidence.

It's more meaningful to dress in a way that makes you feel confident and which feels right for you than to fit in, whether you're overdressed or underdressed, so long as basic levels of decorum, cleanliness and hygiene are observed. People may not understand at first but ultimately they'll realise that you know who you are and you're happy with that – which speaks volumes about your brand. And for anyone who takes a negative view, it's back to what I said on page 23: not everyone will buy your brand so accept that.

PAY ATTENTION TO THE DETAIL

There are of course things for which standing out from the crowd isn't a good idea. They're things which engender a negative reaction from a vast majority of people because they're hardwired into our culture as being less than acceptable (some to a greater extent than others):

- Chewed fingernails (and sometimes fingers)
- Nails so dirty you could grow stuff under them
- Chipped nail polish that's wearing off, rather than taken off
- Very long nails (particularly on a man)
- Fingers stained brown from years of nicotine
- Scuffed shoes, white and cracked with decades of wear
- Worn heels and holes in soles
- Threadbare collar and cuffs, shiny from years of ironing
- Un-ironed shirts that have been 'hung up' on the floor
- Chest hair that creeps up over a collar (particularly on a woman!)
- Missing buttons – especially when they leave too much flesh on show
- Trouser hems frayed from dragging on the ground
- Hair so greasy you could cook chips with it
- A tidemark of roots from long-forgotten hair dying
- Lazy stubble (as opposed to the designer sort)
- A beard hosting the remains of breakfast, lunch and dinner
- Bad breath of the coffee, nicotine, garlic or unidentifiable odour kind
- Unflossed teeth accompanied by unidentifiable food remnants
- Armpits that smell like week-old milk
- Feet that smell like the cheese counter at Waitrose
- Aftershave or perfume that could strip paint
- Reminders of last night's dinner on ties and shirts
- Poorly fitting clothes from a slimmer time
- A snowfall of dandruff
- A slack tie with a sloppy knot
- A less than wholesome tattoo

I did say they were little things – the sort that might look trivial when you see them written down. You might even be thinking, "Well, one or two apply to me but I am who I am, people can take me or leave me." That's fine…but don't be surprised if they choose the latter because, to some, they're absolute deal-breakers.

TATTOO YOU

I thought I'd include a specific note about the last one on the list – tattoos. It's something I get asked about a lot, particularly regarding the effect on someone's career prospects. My answer always starts by asking what sort of career the person wants. In sectors like the media and design, a tattoo is not only accepted without question, it's seemingly de rigueur to have one. In the more traditional sectors like banking and law, uniformity still reigns and if you don't entirely fit the mould you'll only get so far.

Here's what I'm talking about...
I was told about a young guy who deliberately got heavily tattooed so he would never get a 'normal' job in a bank, because that was his idea of failure. He now travels the world as a dancer with a burlesque troupe (although his anti-establishment streak hasn't stopped him getting a pension plan!)

It's definitely changing though. The *Sunday Times* reported that one in five UK adults are estimated to have got inked. As that number continues to rise, across every age range (even veteran broadcaster David Dimbleby has one), we'll see a shift in attitudes. The people currently doing the hiring who are of a mind that tattoos are bad are being replaced by people who themselves have tattoos, so see them in a different light.

We're not there yet though. My advice is, if you're thinking of getting a tattoo, keep your options open and have it on a part of your body where you can choose to cover it or display it. (So none of that Mike Tyson face art then.)

TURN ON OR TURN OFF

When it comes to people buying or not-buying your brand, you never know what someone's particular bug-bear will be.

Here's what I'm talking about...

One executive I know never hires anyone with scuffed shoes, thinking if they can't make an effort for the interview, how much effort will they put into the job? Another client had a meeting with a potential supplier but was put off as soon as he sat down and his ill-fitting shirt gaped to reveal his hairy belly button. And a marketing manager I worked with refused to give a guy a job because he'd worn a tie but had his top button undone behind it. They're little things but with a big impact.

I'm not saying it's fair but those preconceptions are there and although Mother Nature (and a lack of cash for plastic surgery) might stop you altering some of them, it's worth the time and effort on those you can. Even the biggest guy with a well-established beer-gut can look dapper in a made-to-measure shirt; professionally dyed tresses can take years off a lady's age; and everyone comes across better if they're freshly laundered (both them and their clothes). When you think about what it could do to your pay packet, the return on investment is obvious.

DRESS FOR WHERE YOU'RE GOING

Even if you don't have any of those little issues, there's still a lot to be said for taking the occasional step back from your Image and checking out what others see. Sometimes you start your career with one look and, though you've progressed through a promotion or two along the way, you're still dressing as you did in the beginning.

The younger generation are particularly susceptible to this; they've been working for a year or so and the pay packets have been coming in, but they'll still act the pauper and wear the cheap suits and high street fashion they began with on day one. The problem is, by continuing to dress as a student, they continue to be perceived as a student – someone with no workplace knowledge or experience – which isn't doing them justice.

The rule here is to dress for the job you want. It's a cliché, I know, but clichés tend to be so because they contain a lot of truth. Think about someone who's already doing the job you want, or the client you wish to have in your portfolio. Then think about their image – what they wear, their accessories, their body language – to give you an idea of where you should be pitching. As I know from personal experience, you have to speculate to accumulate, so spending some dosh on decent clothes and accessories now will pay dividends later – especially if you land that promotion or bag that new customer. (How else would I justify that new dress?)

WHEN DISTRACTING ISN'T DETRACTING

Someone who can help you take a good look at your Image is a professional stylist. They'll tell you what works on you and what doesn't plus, just as importantly, how to translate your personal brand into your look.

A lot of image styling follows tried and tested rules and while many make sense (let's be honest, tartan trousers with a paisley waistcoat are rarely going to be a winner) there's one I've come across that I disagree with: if it distracts, it detracts.

It's correct that if something is distracting a person's attention it could be detracting from the message you're trying to get across. It's like when someone has something hanging from their nostril and the more they talk the more fascinated you become wondering how long it's going to stick there, so you stop listening to what they're saying. However, I've experienced plenty of times when the thing that's distracting is actually adding to the message. It's giving fantastic clues to the person's brand and communicating more about who they are and what they're all about than words ever could. That's when it's a definite advantage to let your Image do the talking.

Here's what I'm talking about...

An executive once told me about an image consultant who had pointed to the red handkerchief arranged in his top pocket and told him to get rid of it because it was a distraction. He, however, was having none of it, as he'd been wearing a red handkerchief for years and it was now a 'signature piece' that people knew him for. Far from detracting, that one square of cloth conveyed a whole host of clues to his brand: his self-assurance, showmanship and joie de vivre.

DON'T FORGET THE ACCESSORIES

A final note about Image is to remember the accessories because they give just as many clues as your clothing and physique: your mobile (and its cover), laptop, organiser, business card, handbag, wallet, jewellery, watch...even your car. While you're thinking about those, remember one other thing: be consistent.

As I pointed out on page 66, people are picking up clues to your personal brand all the time, in every way, but if you throw them a curve-ball – something that doesn't add up with all the other clues – their brain gets confused and starts to wonder which message they're receiving is the right one. The inconsistency makes them question your personal brand.

Here's what I'm talking about...

When I met Colin for the first time he pulled out a Mont Blanc pen (a clue that quality mattered) and a Moleskine notebook (ditto) before sitting down to chat. When he got up to leave though he handed me a thin, under-sized, poorly printed business card that gave me an entirely different clue: cheap. My brain was left wondering which clue was right and as we'd hit it off so well (a glass of Rioja will do that) I mentioned it. Colin replied, "You know, when those cards turned up I was really disappointed" – a feeling he'd just passed on to me. Needless to say, he trashed them and ordered a new lot.

You'll probably already know what those inconsistencies are because they're the things you feel slightly embarrassed about. Like the guy who said to me, "My mobile looks like it came out of The Ark." Or the woman who noted, "My handbag has seen better days." Or the graduate with a chewed pen who admitted, "It looks disgusting."

My own example of inconsistency was a knackered, old VW Golf I drove in the early days of my business. It had been all I could afford and while the VW brand matched my own, the colour (a rosy apple red with light grey interior) certainly didn't. I knew it didn't make the impression I wanted – hence why I'd park in the furthest corner of my clients' car parks. So if you have something that's not fitting your brand, do something about it. I changed my car as soon as I could afford to and now I'll happily park at the front.

ONE THING EVERY BRAND NEEDS

I've one last tip for improving your Image that every single person can afford: a smile.

According to a study by neuroscientist Andrew Newberg the smile is "the symbol that was rated with the highest positive emotional content. [It] stimulates our brain's reward mechanisms in a way that even chocolate, a well-regarded pleasure inducer, cannot match." And it doesn't seem to matter if the smile comes from us or someone else – we still feel good. Just look at this picture:

Did it make you smile inside, or even on the outside? One of the reasons we feel happy around babies (so long as they're not bawling) is they smile more – 400 times a day on average. Compare that to an average adult, who smiles about 20 times a day, and you'll see why putting a grin on your gob could instantly improve your brand.

Smiling more can take a bit of practice. But if you consciously boost the amount you smile at colleagues then progress to anyone who makes eye contact, even complete strangers, you'll soon find people are smiling back and buy-in to your brand increases.

An added benefit is making yourself smile sends a signal to your brain that you're happy (even if you're not), so your brain cheers up, which makes you smile all the more, which makes you even happier, which makes your brand even more appealing.

Here's what I'm talking about...

I do workshops for an executive group where the deal is, after I've finished, I have to sit at the front and receive immediate feedback, good and bad, without comment...not a peep in response or defence. On one occasion a CEO had taken a dislike to me the instant I'd walked into the room. I know because he told me so at great length during his feedback, along with a host of other negative comments. As I sat there listening to what was wrong with me and my brand, I made sure I had a smile on my face. Partly it was because, while I disagreed with what he was saying, I wanted him to know I was taking it on board. Partly it was because, when you're being torn off a strip in front of a group of male executives, they need to see you're in control and not about to run blubbing from the room. And partly it was because, by putting a smile on my face, I sent a signal to my brain that I was enjoying myself (though there were thousands of places I'd rather have been) which lessened the impact. Well...that and the fact the moment he'd walked into the room I'd taken an instant dislike to him too!

Some Dos and Don'ts about Image

- **DO** pay attention to Image – it's the quickest way people pick up clues to your brand.
- **DO** wear clothes that deliver 'enclothed cognition' to affect your brain in a positive way.
- **DO** consider the little things that may not matter to you but can be others' bug-bears.
- **DON'T** do Dress Down Day if it's not part of your brand.
- **DO** dress for the job/client you want not just the one you have.
- **DON'T** be afraid of wearing something distracting if it's saying something positive.
- **DON'T** forget to pay attention to the accessories.
- **DO** give consistent clues via every single aspect of your Image.

EMAIL

Email is both a blessing and a curse. On one hand it's a great medium to get your personal brand across because you can craft your message before hitting the send button. On the other hand, a poorly worded missive can do more damage than good and be easily forwarded to an even bigger audience, so its impact on your brand shouldn't be taken lightly.

SETTING THE RIGHT TONE

When you email, body language can't factor in the communication; you've only got the words you type and, to some extent, the tone of voice you use to convey your brand message. (Even that's open to interpretation – I mean, have you ever tried using irony in an email?) So you have to make an extra effort with the words to try and redress the balance.

The best way to do that is to write as you'd talk; after all, if you'd say something a certain way on the phone, why change it entirely just because it's written down? (Although you don't have to include the "ums" and "ers" obviously.)

It may seem strange when we've been brought up to believe being professional = being formal, but it's entirely possible to be professional and still have a personality in people's inbox. For instance, instead of beginning your email 'Further to our discussion' start it instead with 'Following our chat'. Or instead of ending your email 'Please do not hesitate to contact me if you have any questions' (which in any case includes negative language in 'hesitate') end it instead with 'Give me a ring if you have any questions'.

It's the same thing you'd say if you'd spoken to the person, so how could it not be professional?

SHOW YOUR SMILE :)

Something that can add a lot to your tone of voice in emails is emoticons – those little smiley/frowning/winking/astonished/ laughing (and depending on your point of view, down right annoying) faces that appear in the text.

For a long time, I was anti-emoticons. As far as I was concerned, they were used by people who wear Hawaiian shirts to be quirky, give colleagues nicknames they don't want and think *Twister* is as much fun as you can have with your clothes on ie a bit of a plonker. However, over the years I've shifted camps and now use emoticons, making every effort to avoid being seen as a plonker myself. One of the things that persuaded me was reading some research.

Here's what I'm talking about...
Professor Nicholas Epley, author of *Mindwise*, asked volunteers to write two different sentences on a variety of topics, one intended to be sarcastic, the other serious. He also asked them whether they thought the recipient would be able to tell which was which. The volunteers were confident that those getting their emails would appreciate when they were being sarcastic, but recipients did no better than they would have done by tossing a coin. Epley's point is that because we know what we mean, we assume others will too.

It's therefore safe to think that anything that adds emotion to a message to convey our intention would be useful. That's when emoticons (coined from the phrase 'emotional icons') can help, though I use a few basic rules that I suggest you consider too:

Rule #1 – Limit the number of emoticons per message

A good aim when writing a message is to do it in such a way that an emoticon isn't even needed. However, when sarcasm or irony creeps in, or you want to emphasise a light-hearted comment, add the relevant symbol. I'd suggest an absolute maximum of two per email, though one is a better limit. That's because you can't be sure the person receiving the message doesn't perceive emoticons and their users as I used to, so any more would exacerbate that.

Rule #2 – Limit the type of emoticons used

On the whole, I'd try sticking to three basic emoticons:

:) Happy
:(Sad
;) Nudge and a wink

That's because a) they offer pretty much all you need on the tone of voice spectrum and b) to use more elaborate ones could give rise to a perception that you're an emoticon aficionado who'll soon be knocking on your recipient's door in a Hawaiian shirt with *Twister* under your arm.

Rule #3 – Limit the people you share emoticons with

Before slipping an emoticon into an email or text, think about the person on the receiving end and their likely response to it based on their own style of communication and the relationship you have. For those with whom, when face-to-face, you share sarcasm/irony/light-hearted banter, feel free to use an emoticon to convey your sarcasm/irony/light-hearted banter. For those with whom you'd be more formal in person, be more formal by email and leave the emoticons out.

SALUTATIONS AND SIGN-OFFS

Another thing that can set the tone of your emails – plus give subtle clues to your brand – is how you begin and end them. There's a difference between saying 'Best wishes' or 'All the best' and 'Warm wishes' or 'Take care'. The word 'best' conveys a leading edge to your brand while 'warm' and 'care' convey a nurturing side. (Although I use 'Cheers' a lot which probably conveys alcoholism.)

You should also temper your email salutations and sign-offs by moving up and down your brandwidth to match the relationship you have with the person, taking into consideration their age, status, communication style, etc.

If it's the first time you've been in touch, you could begin with 'Good morning' or 'Hello' (just as you would if you were introduced in person) and sign off with a formal 'Regards' or 'Sincerely'.

If you've been in conversation for a while though, your opening salvo might be 'Hi there' and your sign-off 'Speak soon' or 'Thanks' (or 'Many thanks' if generosity is part of your brand).

If you're particularly friendly with someone and have had a lot of banter in the past, you could consider going a step further with a 'Howdy' or 'Bonjourno' to start and 'Enjoy the weekend' or 'Hasta La Vista' to end – it's certainly 9½mph language!

> *Here's what I'm talking about...*
> A quick trawl through my inbox revealed a bunch of emails where people had used 'Morning', 'Ey up', 'Hiya' 'Speak soon', 'See ya' and 'Laters'. I even had one that ended 'Have a happy weekend with your chickens', which made the message extra personal and saw me buy into that person's brand just that little bit more.

BUILD RAPPORT

If you really want to make an impression with your email, try to avoid the 10mph "I hope you are well" and instead start with something that will help to built rapport with the recipient. It can be some small personal detail you remember about them, like the fact their wife was expecting a baby (always good to ask if it arrived yet) or they were jetting off to The Alps to go skiing (so check they still have both legs in tact). Or, failing that, pick a current news topic.

Here's what I'm talking about...

During the London Olympics I was emailing a woman I'd met only once before. I started with the words: 'Hi Sharon. I've been working in the office today and after taking some time out to watch Bradley Wiggins win gold, thought I'd drop you a line.' (The rest of the email got straight to the business stuff.) Her reply began: 'If only we were back watching Bradley. I'm trying to work out which sport I can take up to get a gold in Rio and not be too old!' By adding some personality into our emails we found some common ground and got a lot further with our relationship than if we'd stayed formal.

If you're in any doubt about the best tone of voice to use, take your lead from the other person as mirroring someone's language is a great way to build rapport. If they use 'Good morning' or sign off with their initial rather than their full name, doing the same subliminally shows you've paid attention to what they've put and makes them feel 'listened to'. And on that note, one way the people will quickly feel 'not-listened to' is if they get no response at all.

Here's what I'm talking about...

I once sent an email to a group of 35 people who were attending my workshop in a week's time. I introduced myself, provided some pre-session information and said I looked forward to meeting them. Do you know how many replied? Not a single one. Nobody took a few seconds to type six little letters – "Thanks" – let alone, "Thanks and look forward to meeting you too." I don't for an instant think I'm alone in getting this (lack of) response. So imagine how easy it could be for you to stand out from the crowd by simply hitting the reply button and typing a few words.

TAKE TIME TO GET IT RIGHT

Emails are incredibly convenient; you can send a communication quickly, to lots of people at once, at any time of day, and even know if people have read it. (Although I'm not a fan of 'read receipt' as it makes me feel like a naughty child who can't be trusted to do their homework.) Watch out though: with the convenience can come laziness and sloppiness.

Laziness arises when all you do is send emails, as opposed to picking up the phone or walking over to someone's desk, and over time can weaken your personal brand. If people's contact with you is only through the written word, without the extras your tone of voice and body language bring, their ability to 'opt out' of buying your brand is easier. After all, you're just a faceless person sitting in their inbox.

Sloppiness tends to come in the form of a quickly dashed off note that lacks punctuation, spelling or sometimes even complete words (text speak has a lot to answer for). That may be quick for you but when the recipient has to spend time working out your version of a *Countdown Conundrum* they'll soon switch off and go away with a less than favourable view of your brand.

Take time writing your emails and re-read them before hitting the send button. You won't get it 100% right 100% of the time (an ex-colleague of mine still takes great delight in pointing out my occasional errors as I was the one who used to proof-read his communications) but you'll have a better hit rate – and perception of your brand – than if you don't.

IT'S WHAT THEY SEE AS WELL AS READ

When you think of writing an email, you tend to concentrate on the words, but the recipient gets just as many clues from how it looks.

The font you use can speak volumes (quite literally at times if you're SHOUTING IN UPPER CASE!) Serif – those where the letters have 'feet' such as Times New Roman – convey a more traditional, grown-up, serious style, whilst the sans serif fonts – those 'without feet' such as Arial or Calibri – convey a younger, more modern feel. I'd advise against using Comic Sans though as it's a bit too "Way-hay, I'm a fun person" for many and you'll come across as a muppet.

Here's what I'm talking about...

In an April Fool's mickey-take, CERN (those clever boffins who run the Hadron Collider) changed its website font to Comic Sans. It was because, according to the news release, "This is a serious research laboratory with a serious agenda. And it makes the letters look all round and squishy." Seems physicists have a sense of humour after all.

Your email footer is another place people will pick up on your brand, so use it to your advantage. If you have a company logo, consider including it to add a visual element. If you have a website, or you're on LinkedIn, Twitter or Facebook (for business purposes, not social) include a link to each. If you write a blog, have had a bit of media coverage or are running an event, consider including a message about that with another link.

I've also seen people include a famous quotation – something that means a lot to them and therefore gives a clue to their brand (although beware of being too schmaltzy). And as the whole premise of branding is that people buy people, including a small photo of you can work too. (I stress the word 'small'– if your photo's too big it will scream 'egomaniac'.)

You could also choose to have a scan of your signature appear instead of just typing your name. It's a lovely, personal touch and your handwriting will itself give hints to who you are. A word of warning though: if the recipient's email system blocks images, they'll end up with a blank space and your message will finish without your name.

Don't forget to set up the email footers on your mobile or tablet too. Personalising it is a must and useful if you want to make it clear you're typing on the move so messages may be short or contain the odd typo. Remember people will pick up clues from what you write so keep it professional.

> ### Here's what I'm talking about...
> One recruiter I know decided against interviewing a candidate when he read the guy's email sign off: Brought to you by Lard Arse Productions.

Finally, don't forget the email address itself. I've seen plenty of people give revealing clues just from their choice of username, creating a whole host of preconceptions that aren't necessarily positive.

There are those using their year of birth as part of the address with potentially ageist results, like davejones1951@hotmail.com. Or the people using their partner's nickname for them who take informality too far, like snugglebum@gmail.com. Or the ones describing their social-life as a badge of honour, like partyboy@yahoo.com. Or those whose emails sound like they should be on a postcard in a phone box in a dodgy area of town, like bustyblondebombshell@hotmail.com. (OK, maybe I haven't seen anything quite like that but I figured I'd better warn you just in case you were thinking of something similar!)

AUTO REPLY

Holidays...when thoughts turn to where you've stashed those bamboo beach mats and whether you can squeeze another year out of that bottle of mosquito repellent. Before you head out the door and into your flip flops though, there's an important part of your personal brand to consider: the out of office message (OOO).

Though you won't be around in person, with a little thought you can still be working your brand magic even when you're not there (and that goes for whenever you're away from your desk for prolonged periods).

Here's what I'm talking about...

One CEO I had as a client gave some great clues to the fact he was hard-working, driven and committed to his job with a message that read, 'I'm out of the office until 2 June having been persuaded to take a family holiday. However, I'll have my mobile with me and will be delighted to speak to you if your enquiry is urgent.' (Not sure his wife was quite so delighted though.)

The first thing to remember is to write your OOO message in the same way as you would if you were there to reply to the email in person. There's still someone at the other end who'll be reading it, so do them the courtesy of including a salutation (something like 'Hi there' or 'Thanks for your email' works as you won't know what time of day it is) and sign it with your name.

Here's what I'm talking about...

A lesson in how not to do it. One executive I knew who regularly used his OOO to set out his week had a message that read 'Monday: London, Tuesday: Head Office, Wednesday: Leeds, Thursday: Ops Centre, Friday: day off. Call my PA with any queries.' The irony was this guy had a really welcoming brand in person, but was leaving readers feeling as if they'd been barked at by a drill sergeant instead.

Don't forget though, your OOO is a prime opportunity to communicate something about your personal brand and offer a relationship hook to help people connect with you. For instance, I once received an OOO from a contact which included the line, 'I'm away walking in the Lake District and will return on...' It worked a treat because a) I hadn't known he was into hill walking b) I enjoy walking in The Dales so found we had something in common and c) it gave me a great relationship hook to start a conversation when I next spoke to him.

Even if you're not going on holiday, you can still create a message that's going 9½mph and actually gives clues to your brand: 'I'll be expanding my mind at the IT Expo in London...' (which suggests you enjoy learning) or 'I'll be spending the day working on a project with my team...' (which suggests you're a team player). So don't ignore the humble OOO.

Some Dos and Don'ts about Email

- **DO** write your emails as you would when speaking to the person.
- **DO** write a salutation and sign-off that matches your relationship.
- **DO** start your email with something personal to build rapport.
- **DON'T** hit the send button without checking spelling and grammar.
- **DO** consider how your email looks as well as reads.
- **DON'T** choose an email address that sends the wrong signals.
- **DO** use your out of office to promote your brand even when you're not there.

LETTERS

Writing a letter to a business contact is becoming a rare thing (I'm talking individual letters, not those mailshots that litter the doormat) – so why not use that in your favour? If personal branding is about standing out from the crowd, sending someone a letter through the post would certainly do the trick.

FIRST CLASS DELIVERY

A lot of what there is to say about conveying your brand by letter is already covered in the section on emails: avoid the formal business writing, replicate how you speak, begin on a personal note and take the time to get the spelling and punctuation right. However, there are some things to consider that are exclusive to a letter:

Typing or writing?

My preferred style, particularly if it's a long letter, is to type the body of the letter but hand write the salutation and sign-off so it remains personal. However, if you have clear, ordered handwriting that speaks volumes about your brand, go ahead and use it all the way through.

What pen?

It's often the case that the better quality pen you use, the better your handwriting appears, so bear that in mind. If you're a fountain-pen kind of person, use one, or if a biro better reflects your brand, use that instead.

What colour ink?

Yes, even your choice of ink colour could be giving people clues to your personal brand. You may want to go the traditional route with black or blue, but if you've a more colourful character think about reflecting that with something like purple or turquoise. (I'd avoid red as it's associated with marking errors and green is often the colour of choice for people who like to complain – at least it was when I worked for a water company.)

Stamp or frank?

The use of a stamp re-iterates the fact this is a personal letter. Interestingly, a marketing guru I once heard said it's good to put the stamp at a slight angle as people know it's been put on by human hand and not just a machine. (It's a trick he used on mailshots for a charity, which had the effect of increasing donations.)

What paper?

I'd suggest nothing below 100gsm (that's printers' jargon for the thickness of the paper) and preferably something heavier, because you'd be surprised how people pick up on these things. I've even seen people subconsciously stroking the paper when I've printed my workshop handouts on 120gsm.

What envelope?

At the very least your envelope should be as good quality as the paper and preferably a direct match. If you want to have a bit more impact, try something fancier, like a coloured envelope.

SHOW YOUR COURTEOUS SIDE

Letters don't just have to be about business. A great way to make a positive impact and gain that extra little bit of buy-in is to use them as a thank-you. A handwritten note following a meeting (and particularly an interview) that thanks the person for their time, talks about what you got out of it and says you look forward to hearing from them works wonders – especially if you send it soon after you've met.

Here's what I'm talking about...

One person I know carries around paper and envelopes so he can write the note immediately following the meeting and post it the same day. Not only does it convey his courtesy it also conveys how organised he is.

Or for a more modern twist, you could use an app like Touchnote to send a postcard from your phone.

Some Dos and Don'ts about Letters

- **DO** consider using a letter to really stand out from the communication crowd.
- **DO** think not only about the words you're writing but what you're writing on and with.
- **DON'T** use a franking machine but **DO** use a stamp.
- **DO** send a short, handwritten note to important contacts to strengthen their buy-in.

TELEPHONE

The benefit of the telephone over email is you can deliver a more personal facet to your brand; your language will be freer and your tone of voice will convey a lot more than words alone. So whenever you're trawling through your inbox and hitting the reply button, consider hitting the dial button instead.

MAKE SURE THEY HEAR YOU SMILE

It's an old sales technique to slap a smile on your face before you pick up the receiver because the person at the other end will hear it in your voice and get a positive impression of you. Another tip is to stand up to make important calls, with your shoulders back and your feet planted firmly on the ground, so the confidence of your stance comes across in your voice.

My personal tip builds on those and ties into the enclothed cognition theory explained on page 90 and it's this: dress for the call. Just as smiling will make you more upbeat and standing will make you more confident, if you're dressed as you would to meet the person face-to-face you'll come across just as professional. However, if you're under-dressed (or even undressed) just because you're on the phone, you'll end up sending a very different message. I should know…the one time I carried out a call dressed in my slouching gear (washed-out jogging bottoms and shapeless T-shirt plus unwashed hair) I was so conscious I wasn't being the 'me' they'd meet in person, I couldn't get my words straight and sounded like a right pillock.

DON'T FORGET THE VOICEMAIL

Just like your out of office message, your voicemail is a key way to get your brand across even when you're not there, so don't ignore it.

Let me set the scene: Bill and Jim are having a meeting when Bill says, "I've a great opportunity for a project manager – the sort of thing that can make a person's career – and I'm looking for someone who's really dynamic, pays attention detail and is confident enough to take control. But it's proving harder than I thought to find someone who's different from the same-old, same-old. Can you recommend anyone?" Jim replies, "I know just the person – you need to speak to Jo Green…she fits the bill exactly. Here's her mobile number."

First of all, Jo should get a gold star for having a brand reputation that delivers even when she's not in the room – but depending on her voicemail that could all go by the wayside.

Let's start with scenario #1: Bill calls the number Jim gave him and gets the standard voicemail message from Jo's provider – something along the lines of, "This is the O2 voicemail messaging service for 07867…"

This could have a number of effects. It could make Bill feel nervous (a common reaction is to wonder if you dialled the wrong number), which isn't a great thing to have associated with your brand. It could make Bill feel annoyed (I know plenty of people who won't leave a message if they get an un-personalised voicemail). Or it could leave Bill wondering how much attention to detail Jo would pay to his project if she can't even pay attention to her message. Whichever reaction Bill has, it's possible he'll simply erase Jo from his list of prospects.

In scenario #2, Bill calls and gets a personalised message but it's the one that's used by the majority of people, "I'm sorry I can't take your call but please leave a message and I'll get back to you."

Firstly, the apology sends a subconscious message to Bill's brain: "She's apologising…she must have done something wrong," which creates an unnecessarily negative view. (Worse still is saying "I'm afraid I can't take your call" or "Sadly I can't take your call" – what are you afraid of/sad about?) Secondly, giving a same-old, same-old message portrays Jo as a same-old, same-old person. Plus if it's been recorded in a lacklustre voice that sounds like Jo's about as interesting as toothache, Bill will get no hint of the dynamism Jim said she had. Again, a bad result and a missed opportunity.

In scenario #3, Bill calls the number and not only gets a personalised voicemail message, but a real feel for Jo's brand. He hears a high-energy voice say, "Hi, this is Jo Green. I'm busy right now but I'll be sure to get back to you as soon as I can. Thanks."

Her attention to detail has come across in the fact she's recorded a distinctive message (not same-old, same-old), her dynamism has come across in her voice, and her confidence and taking control are borne out with the words "I'll be sure to", which have entered Bill's subconscious in a very positive way.

Bill's impressed, leaves a message, Jo phones him back (just as she said she would), they have a chat and it's the beginning of a great working relationship.

The moral of the story? For people to buy into your brand they have to trust what they're buying into and something as simple as a voicemail message can make or break that.

GET RECORDING

I do understand why so many people stick to the standard voicemail message. It's because the majority of people don't like the sound of their own voice (talk-radio DJs excepted) and the prospect of having to hear it on their phone is just too horrible to contemplate. But as you've just read, there's potentially a lot at stake if you don't, so man-up and let's get to work:

Step 1 – Compose your message

It's a lot easier to record a good voicemail if you know what you need to say, so write it down beforehand. It's a simple tip but we all know people whose messages include lots of "uh" and "um" as they lose their train of thought. It also gives you the ability to compose something a bit more 9½mph than just "Leave me a message and I'll get back to you." (Though please don't do what one person I know did by recording, "Unless you've got something interesting to say, don't bother leaving a message.") Better still, include a clue to your brand.

Here's what I'm talking about...
My voicemail includes the line, "I promise I'll return your call when I get your message." The word 'promise' gives a clue to my #1 brand value – delivering what I say I will – and even though it's subtle it gets picked up; one caller left a message saying, "You've promised to return my call so you better bloody well had!" As an alternative, a client whose brand is empathetic and caring says, "I'd love to speak to you so please leave a message." Another who enjoys building relationships says, "I really look forward to speaking to you." A contact who always has a huge smile on her face ends with, "Have a lovely day!" And another whose brand is built around his deep respect for others has the words, "I really value your call," which fits entirely with who he is.

Remember though: the shorter you can keep your composition the easier it will be for you to say it without running out of breath and turning blue in the face.

Step 2 – Pick your time and place

It's hard enough to record a good voicemail message without making it worse by doing it on the hop, rushing from pillar to post, with lots of noise in the background. Instead, find somewhere quiet where you won't be interrupted (like the toilet), with decent acoustics (hmm, maybe not the toilet then), when you have at least 10 minutes to spare so you can take your time.

Step 3 – Stand up and smile

As you want to sound the same as if you've answered the phone in person, some of the tips from earlier still apply: stand up when you do the recording and slap a smile on your face before you start. You'll also need to add some extra energy into your voice that you wouldn't in a normal conversation; recordings have a funny way of dampening down the vocal when played back, so you have to ramp it up to compensate. One way to do that is to bounce on the balls of your feet as you do the recording (so long as you don't end up heavy breathing – you're not running a sex line).

Step 4 – Keep going until you get it right

The bottom line is you want a voicemail that sounds exactly as you would if you had picked up the phone, so if you listen back and still don't think the recording is doing you justice, start again. (I took 12 attempts to get mine right.)

RING-A-DING-DING

For those of you who use your mobile phone for work, remember that the sound of your ringtone sends very audible clues to your brand. (After all, I'm sure we've all been on a train, heard someone's ringtone and without even seeing whose it is know full well the person's a complete prat.)

You might convey a retro feel with the sound of a 70s Trimphone, a sense of fun with the theme tune from Benny Hill, or some gravitas with a bit of Beethoven's Fifth. There's no right or wrong, so long as you've consciously thought about what you want to get across.

Here's what I'm talking about...

Speaking at a seminar one morning, I illustrated the clues a ringtone can give by playing a short clip then asking the audience what they associated with it. After hearing 10 seconds of *Gangnam Style* by Psy, the majority view was that it was used by party animals who were as annoying as the music itself. Then one lady stuck up her hand to say she had that precise ringtone, but only because her teenage kids had put it on her phone. She'd never considered what people might presume about her personal brand from such a (supposedly) inconsequential thing, but she'd be changing it...fast!

TEXTING

While we're on the subject of phones, I'll finish with a quick thought about texting. You may or may not use it much for business, but if you do, I'd advise against heavy usage of text-speak. Your ALOL, WFM, MRA, TSTB and RTBM might mean something to you, but you can't be certain it will mean anything to the recipient (apart from them thinking you have little grasp of English).

Take time to type your usual shorthand in its longer version, or better still, just call them instead. And in case you're wondering, those acronyms mean: 'Actually laughing out loud', 'Works for me', 'Moving right along', 'The sooner the better' and 'Read the bloody manual'.

Some Dos and Don'ts about the Telephone
- **DO** pick up the phone – it's more personal and you can convey things you can't in an email.
- **DO** record a personalised voicemail that sounds just as you would if you'd answered the phone.
- **DO** give people clues to your personal brand by choosing specific words to include in your message.
- **DO** think about what your ringtone conveys.
- **DON'T** use text speak for business messages.

MEETINGS

Of all the ways you interact in the office, meetings are possibly the best in terms of giving personal brand clues, because you have the full monty of communication tools coming together at once: your words, your voice and your body language. The person-to-person interaction is also great for building relationships as the chatting can flow more easily than by phone, email or text.

JUST BECAUSE

Whilst meetings are near the top of the charts when it comes to opportunities to blow your personal brand trumpet, I often come across a reticence to use them for anything other than business as usual; people are happy to talk about the matter in hand but not what matters to them.

If you're in that camp I'm going to give you a gift. It's a single word that will make talking about your brand in meetings as easy as talking about the weather:

'Because'

Simply pop it onto the end of a sentence about what you do and give people an insight into why you do it, or how you do it, or who you are when you do it (or any other aspect of your brand). So when you've said what you've said simply add on something like:

- "…because I want to make a difference to others."
- "…because I'm good at seeing trends."
- "…because I've taken an optimistic view."
- "…because I think it's better to be straight about things."
- "…because I want to be fair to the team."
- "…because I have a knack for asking the right questions."
- "…because I see the potential and want to challenge people."

Here's what I'm talking about...

A newly-promoted HR Director was finding it hard to define what he brought to the board table until we discovered his key Driver was brokering the interests of the staff (which were often overlooked by his sales-focused peers). That was fine and dandy until I said, "Now you need to share that with everyone else." He replied, "How am I going to do that? I can't just rock up to a Board meeting and say, 'I'm the voice of the staff'." So I explained that all he had to do was use 'because' and let it flow from there. To give him an example I asked if he ever had to present a Board paper along the lines, "We had problem A, I came up with solutions B and C, and after a full evaluation I chose option C." He said he did. I suggested he simply add on "...because it matters to me that the staff have a voice in this," or "...because I believe it offered the best outcome for the staff as well as the company," or "...because my position on this is to get the balance of sales and staff welfare." He was comfortably giving clues to what made him tick simply by explaining his decision.

Of course you don't have to save 'because' for meetings – you can pop it on the end of anything, whether over the phone or in an email.

BODY TALK

As I said earlier, meetings have the benefit of adding body language into the communication mix, even when you're not aware it's saying anything. It's doing the lion's share of the talking, so pay attention to it – because everybody else will be.

Here's what I'm talking about...

Delivering a workshop to a group of graduates one day, I pointed out to one that he had yawned six times in the first half hour. At first he thought I was joking because, as far as he was aware, he hadn't yawned once. After convincing him it was indeed true, he was gobsmacked. "I had no idea I looked bored...I'm really enjoying the session!"

Building on the positive spoken language you'll be using (you paid attention on page 81 didn't you?) show consistency by using positive body language too. That means sitting with your butt all the way back in your chair, so your spine is supported and upright – as opposed to sitting with your butt near the front of the chair so you end up slumped like a teenager forced to eat at the dinner table. (Slumping has the added disadvantage of making you look shorter, which won't be helping your presence.)

It also means putting your shoulders back and lifting your jaw up slightly, instead of doing your impression of the Hunchback of Notre Dame.

And it means pulling the chair in so you can comfortably put your elbows on the table, maybe even with your fingers interlaced or resting either side of your notepad, so you're staking your place and showing you're an active participant in the meeting. It's also a good position from which to lean in slightly when you have something to say and to look around the table to make eye contact.

On that point: remember that every person at the table is your audience, even if some are more important to you than others, so don't just focus your gaze on the head honcho when you speak. It's likely to be noticed and will either make you look like a toadying suck-up or at the very least someone who's not exactly got inclusivity at the heart of their brand.

You're not going to be talking all the time though are you? Using positive body language also means showing you're listening; as they say, there's a reason you have two ears and only one mouth (although we've got 10 fingers so perhaps what we're really meant to do is poke people!) Making eye contact with the person speaking, smiling when something they say makes a lot of sense and gently nodding to show you agree are all good ways to do that.

Here's what I'm talking about...

A woman whose personal brand was of the quiet, reflective sort told me she found it hard to get heard in meetings. I asked her to show me how she sat in those situations and she pushed her chair back slightly, leant back and placed her hands in her lap. Everything she'd done said she was listening, not participating. So I asked her to pull her chair in, place her arms on the table, lean slightly forwards and raise one arm at a 45° angle whilst loosely pointing with her index finger...as if she was about to say something. All of a sudden, she looked like a woman worth listening to. I suggested she add a verbal "May I...?" at a decent volume and look around to make some eye contact and she'd soon find people would make way for her in the conversation.

MIRROR DON'T MIMIC

Body language is also useful in meetings for building rapport – particularly if you're in a one-to-one. By paying attention to someone's posture, movements, eye contact and facial expressions, you can get some insight into what they're thinking and how much buy-in you've got for your brand.

Be careful about making wrong assumptions though. In his book *What Every Body is Saying*, ex-FBI agent Joe Navarro says it's a myth that there are clear cut ways to interpret certain gestures. Someone touching their nose when they're talking doesn't automatically mean they're lying and someone with their arms crossed doesn't automatically mean they're feeling defensive. (I used to cross my arms in my boss's office simply because he'd have the air conditioning on and I didn't want to embarrass myself when things got perky.)

The body language you can rely more readily on is the stuff where the person sitting opposite you is mirroring what you're doing. If you have both feet planted firmly on the ground, leaning forward with your elbows on your knees and they're doing the same, you can take it as read that there's a fair amount of rapport going on. But if you're in the same position and the other person is leaning back in their chair with their legs stretched and ankles crossed then it looks like you've got some relationship building to do.

To help you do that, consider changing your body language to subtly mirror the other person. The emphasis is on the word 'subtle' there. Anything more than that and you risk looking like one of those mime acts where one matches the other one's every move, which isn't going to win you any friends. So if the other person is sitting forward and you're sitting back, start by getting more upright then slowly take yourself forward as the conversation goes on. If they take a sip of water, take a sip of yours soon after. If they have their arms on the table, put your arms on the table. You'll be reducing the differences between you, both physically and mentally.

Here's what I'm talking about...

I was once interviewed by a panel of three people and was able to gauge how it was going by looking at their body language. The guy in the middle was mirroring me exactly and the woman, although not quite as in tune, was sitting forward and nodding her head, so I was pretty sure I'd won them round. The other guy, however, was reclining in his seat, hands behind his head with an expression that said, "Impress me." I still spoke to and made eye contact with the others, but I subtly turned my body in his direction and gently mirrored his posture, putting my right elbow over the back of my chair and leaning back in a more feminine version of his position. Over time he took his arms down, sat up in his chair and became more attentive, even smiling at times. They didn't offer me the job (we all knew from the first few seconds I wasn't a good fit) but I went away with a lot more brand buy-in than I might have.

One last word on body language: as I said on page 98, a smile goes a very long way in creating a positive personal brand, so turn up the corners of your mouth – in a genuine way, not like some creepy psychopath. Even when you're having a difficult conversation, maybe delivering some criticism or being on the receiving end, you'll find it lessens the sting. Plus you'll feel better and people will feel good about you.

Some Dos and Don'ts about Meetings

- **DO** see meetings as prime time to subtly promote your brand – people can pick up clues from the full monty of communication tools: your words, your voice and your body language.
- **DO** use 'because' as an effective way to get your personal brand across along with the business as usual.
- **DO** use positive body language to match your spoken language.
- **DON'T** forget to listen – it's a big part of communication.
- **DO** mirror people's body language but **DON'T** mimic it.
- **DO** smile.

TIMEKEEPING

Timekeeping comes in many forms – from you physically turning up to appointments when expected, to responding to communications in a timely manner, to meeting your own and others' deadlines. It's something that sends multiple signals about your personal brand to your audiences.

WATCH THE CLOCK

As we've just been talking about meetings, I'll start there, because as well as creating the right impression in the meeting, you need to create the right one getting there.

Many people take timekeeping seriously, leaving plenty of time to get to their destination and, if they look like they're going to be late, will notify the necessary people. All good stuff.

There's a second type of person though who is about as likely to look at a clock as they are to ride a unicorn, or even if they do, seem to have an inability to relate the time shown to their working day. They know they have a meeting at 10am but take that as a 'suggested' time. They don't leave their desk until the big hand is well past the 12, then saunter into the room with a "Sorry I'm late" spoken in a tone which conveys the real meaning – "You're lucky I'm here."

The #1 signal bad timekeeping sends about your brand is that you believe your time is more valuable than anybody else's. That's quickly followed by the implication that you're disorganised and/ or uninterested...none of which is great for getting buy-in from your audience. More than that, bad timekeeping really winds people up so when you do arrive the other person is already in a negative state of mind – not great for building rapport. If you're a persistent offender who's serious about their personal brand you'd better make some changes.

Of course, we live in modern times and the odd delay is expected, but if you handle it well you can still come away with your personal brand halo in place.

> **Here's what I'm talking about...**
> I was driving to an appointment and according to my sat nav's predictions was going to arrive late. I hadn't met the guy before and didn't want that to be his first impression of me so I called up and said, "I understand your time is valuable so I wanted to let you know I'm going to be about 10 minutes late, because I hate keeping people waiting." (See how I slipped that little word 'because' in the middle?) He thanked me for letting him know and said at least he could be doing something useful until I arrived. Even though being late was a negative thing, I'd turned it into a positive and sold a bit of my brand on the way.

MANAGE EXPECTATIONS

It's not just when you're running late for a meeting that a bit of 'expectation management' goes down well – it's the same for your emails and voicemail too. Let me ask you a question...and I'd like you to answer it honestly (although we'll do away with the polygraph test):

- Do you currently have an email in your inbox that you should have replied to by now? (I'm talking where it's been more than a couple of days since you received it.)
- Or a voicemail sitting on your phone from someone you should have called back?
- Or a date to be set for a meeting with someone you should have met by now?
- Or a deadline by which you said you'd get back to someone but you haven't?

Why haven't you responded yet?

Looking at it from your side of the table, it probably has something to do with other priorities, full-on workloads and looming deadlines. Those all seem pretty legitimate reasons…but have you even told the other person that's why you have yet to respond?

Now let's look at it from the other side of the table using what I'm pretty certain is a scenario we've all experienced: waiting in for a repairman.

You've had to take the day off work and are now sitting there in limbo, wanting to get on with something but feeling you can't get started because that'll be the moment they choose to turn up. But despite being told they'll arrive some time between 8am and 1pm, it's now well past 2pm and the guy is still a no-show. If you're anything like me, you could be thinking any number of things:

- They're useless at turning up so they're probably useless at their job too.
- They're selfish and have no regard for the fact other people have work to do.
- They're going to take up even more of my time chasing them to sort this out.
- They're rude and didn't even have the decency to call.
- They don't know their arse from their elbow when it comes to doing business.
- They can't be trusted.

All are negative responses that are damaging that company's brand – and we can be sure you'll be telling all your friends about it, so that damage will be spreading further. Now what's the difference between that and the damage you're doing to your personal brand from your own lack of response?

It takes five seconds to manage someone's expectations. Even a simple reply to say, 'I'm really busy right now but I'll get back to you as soon as I can,' will do wonders for keeping your reputation intact. (Although using it as a stalling tactic and then never getting back to the person at all will annihilate it.)

Here's what I'm talking about...

I worked with a CEO who never – and I mean never – returned my calls, even though his voicemail clearly said, "I can't take your call but leave a message and I'll get back to you." When I asked what the deal was he said, "Oh, I never listen to my messages." He's a busy guy, so that's understandable, but it was damaging his brand (I wasn't the only one to mention it). So we changed his voicemail and now you'll hear, "Hi this is John Smith. I don't listen to my voicemails so if you want to get in touch please send me a text or email." It's not the conventional message but it manages expectations and, with it, his brand.

So go on...take half an hour to reply to those emails, voicemails and meeting contacts, even if it's to say you can't get back to them properly yet. The time will be well spent if it stops you getting a reputation as bad as a dodgy repairman's.

Some Dos and Don'ts about Timekeeping

- **DON'T** be a persistently bad timekeeper – it sends the message you think your time is more valuable than everyone else's (plus you're disorganised and/or uninterested).
- **DO** apologise if you're running late and use it as an opportunity to promote your brand.
- **DO** manage expectations but **DON'T** use that as an excuse to ignore the person completely.

CHIT CHAT

And so to our final section on tooting your horn in the office: chit chat. It's something that might seem to have little sway over how your personal brand is perceived by others but is actually another opportunity to get your message across.

FINE...AND DANDY

You're walking down the corridor, meet a colleague, they smile and say "Hi" then follow it up with the words "How are you?" What do you say? If you're using the standard response for the UK, you'll reply "Fine thanks" (very likely followed by the phrase "How are you?")

Not very 9½mph is it? Plus what clues are you giving them to your brand? That it's 'fine', 'OK', 'so-so', 'meh' – not very compelling, eh?

More to the point, if that's your response every time you're asked it's not very authentic either, because it's highly unlikely you'll be fine all the time; sometimes you'll be better than that, sometimes worse.

Your aim should be to stand out from the crowd a little more by giving a response that gets a response, or at the very least gives the person asking something interesting to listen to. If you're feeling great say, "I'm feeling great thanks." If you're feeling fantastic say, "I'm feeling fantastic thanks." If you're having a good day say, "I'm having a good day thanks." And even if you're having a bad day say, "I'm not having a great day but I'm getting there." (Note I still used positive language.)

You could of course use your answer to give a positive clue to your brand. I know someone who has as part of her brand the fact she loves to be busy and gets a real sense of achievement from getting jobs done. If you call her at the office and ask how she is she'll often reply, "I'm having a fab morning thanks – I've ticked loads of things off my to-do list!" You can hear the enthusiasm in her voice that makes for a much more uplifting answer than "Fine thanks" and portrays her as someone who gets things done.

Here's what I'm talking about...

One executive I know has optimism at the heart of his personal brand – he's definitely a 'silver lining' kind of guy. When he's having a particularly good day and someone asks, "Hi Tom, how are you?" he'll say, "I'm happy as a pig in shit." (Even the shit is good for something!) It's an unexpected answer that elicits a smile and gives people a bit of insight into what makes him tick.

THE WALLS HAVE EARS

One thing to realise about chit chat is that it often gets heard by people other than who you're talking to and they'll pick up just as many clues to your brand as the intended recipient – so pay attention! A friend of mine learnt, even though he'd much rather not have, that a female colleague was "Off for my smear test now!" And a member of staff who worked for an MD I know did nothing for her career when she was overheard advising a colleague how to get a pay rise with the words, "If you whine long enough they'll just give in."

Some Dos and Don'ts about Chit Chat

- **DO** remember that even the answer to the question "How are you?" is an opportunity to promote your brand.
- **DON'T** tell people you're "Fine" because that's all people will think of your brand...it's 'fine'.
- **DO** reflect how you're feeling in your answer – give a response that gets a response.
- **DON'T** assume it's only the person you're talking to who'll hear your chit chat.

PROMOTING YOUR BRAND: OUT AND ABOUT

Right…you've got the office covered and no matter how your colleagues and clients are coming into contact with your personal brand, you're giving them an á la carte experience of your signature dish. Now it's time to get your feet out from under your desk as we talk about tooting your horn when you're out and about.

EVENTS

Events are a great opportunity to do just that – whether you're at a workshop, conference, corporate shindig or networking do. If you're anything like me though the thought of having to walk into a room of gregarious people who all know each other, sharing their private jokes and displaying their intellectual prowess, will get you as hot and bothered as a middle-aged woman in need of HRT. I have to really steel myself to do it. However, it's become a lot easier since I've realised something: my perception is complete twaddle. Pretty much everybody in that room is as nervous as I am (save for a few who are blessed with a natural ability to mingle).

Knowing that, and the fact going to events can actually do your career or business a world of good, has changed my approach. Now when I rock up to a do I've already worked out my plan of action: I'll get my name badge, pick up my drink, wander over to the first person who's free and say, "Hi, I'm Jennifer – may I join you?" Guess what? They always say "Yes". Not, "No, you're too stupid," or "No, I don't like the look of you." "Yes". Then they ask me a question, I answer it, the conversation builds and suddenly we look like those gregarious people who seemed so intimidating in the first place.

THE COMPANY YOU KEEP

There are plenty of workshops you can go on to learn how to network (if you can get over the fear of going in the first place) so I won't go into any more tactics. What I will say is it's worth being selective about the events you attend; think about who else will be there, because if you're going to get buy-in to your brand you want it be from the right people. (I once went to a networking event more akin to a seedy singles-night, where it seemed the aim was to 'pick up' as many people as possible then brag about the number of business cards you'd got, like notches on a bedpost.)

Once you're in the room, it's important to get your brand across to people loud and clear. It's likely you'll be meeting a fair few of them for the first time and initial impressions will be paramount, so let's cover a few of the bases…

HANDSHAKES

A big factor in someone's first impression of your brand will be your handshake. They'll gather tons of clues about who you are from this simple gesture and base a lot of their buy-in on what they experience. It's incredible the impact a handshake has, but why do so many people get it wrong?

Based on my many years' experience of attending events, here are some of the bad handshakes I've had the misfortune to experience:

The Fish Fingers

This happens when the person doesn't fully engage with your hand and you're left shaking their fingers, which they hold limply like a dead fish. If you're really unlucky, that fish is still a little wet – not nice! The message I get from that: if they're shy, their lack of confidence comes through or if they seem confident it conveys a certain disdain (like shaking your hand is the last thing they want to do).

Here's what I'm talking about...
I was interviewing people for a press officer's job and needed someone with a thick skin and a lot of confidence who could deal with difficult journalists. I met Lucie in reception, offered my hand and got the weakest handshake going, leading me to think she was way too wishy-washy for what I needed. Turned out I was wrong. As she answered my questions I realised this young woman had steeliness and drive that was perfect for the job. She ended up being one of the best press officers I'd ever had, but I'd never have known it from her handshake.

The Bone Crusher

When the person (most often a man) grips your hand so hard you're left with numb fingers, you've met a Bone Crusher. For one person I knew that proved to be literal as the guy fractured the bone in her finger. The message I get: either they're blissfully unaware of what they're doing or it's their way of saying, "I'm a man and you're not." Well thanks, but I'd already worked that one out.

The Cupper

This happens when the person shakes your hand but cups their palm so that it doesn't actually touch yours. Again, that gives a certain sense of disdain, like they want as little of your skin touching them as possible.

The Double Hander

A favourite of politicians the world over, the Double Hander takes their left hand and puts it on top of the existing handshake. The style is one of sincerity, but the message is clear: I'm in charge here.

The Limpet

The Limpet's hand stays stuck to your hand long after social decorum dictates. It's not often I get this but when I do I find it very disconcerting, wondering where the hand-holding is going to lead (often it's to the 'pull in and kiss on the cheek' – more of which later).

SHAKE IT TO MAKE IT

If that's how to get it wrong, how should you get it right?

Tip #1 – Mean it

I've met shed-loads of people who tell me they hate shaking hands. Reasons vary from "I'm not very good at it," to "I just don't like touching people," to "I've got sweaty hands and I don't want people getting a bad impression." (On that last one, I have it on good authority that a product called TiteGrip could be the answer. It's an antiperspirant for hands used by people who do 'pole work' – and I don't think they're referring to scaffolders.)

They're all reasons I understand but they tend to get overruled by the fact people are going to want to shake hands with you and turning down a proffered palm will cause a darned sight more damage to their feelings than yours.

My advice is to accept that shaking hands is part of life, so approach it as if you mean business. A positive attitude will lead to a much better handshake and, with it, first impression.

Tip #2 – Aim for the crook of the thumb

When you get a limp handshake going on it's often because you haven't linked hands properly in the first place. Your aim should be to get the crook of your thumb (the curve that runs between the base of your thumb and forefinger) interlinked with the crook of their thumb. If you do that, you'll be perfectly placed for the next bit.

Tip #3 – Hold don't grip

Wrap your fingers around their hand – enough to feel you're holding it but not so much as you're gripping it. The ideal is an even pressure from both your thumb and fingers (sometimes people press too hard with one or the other) that matches your brand. If you're a gentler type of person, your hold should be firm but gentle, whereas if you're a stronger character it should be firm and strong.

Then all that's left to do is to shake your hand up and down two or three times and release. Don't be too vigorous though; you want a gentle shake, like getting the last few drops from a wine bottle, not huge jerks like when you start a new bottle of ketchup.

Here's what I'm talking about...
Whilst talking to some workshop attendees about handshakes, I asked a young lady to show me how she did it. She grabbed my hand and with her arm poker-straight gave one sharp jerk like she was cracking a whip. I winced (as did the people watching) as my shoulder nearly left its socket. When I queried her technique, she said, "But that's how it's done." I soon put her right, before she put someone in hospital!

Tip #4 – Eye contact

The final flourish to a good handshake is eye contact – coupled with a beaming smile – that lets the person know you're the real deal and have nothing to hide. You can have the strongest handshake in the world, but if you're looking over the person's shoulder when you're giving it you might as well have not bothered.

Tip #5 – Get it right

Such is the importance of a handshake, getting it wrong could set your personal brand off on the wrong track in someone's mind. So if you muck it up, there's a lot to be said for asking to do it again.

Here's what I'm talking about...
I once did a really bad handshake with a guy and not wanting that to be his first impression of my brand said, "Ooh, that wasn't a very good handshake I gave you – could we try again?" He laughed and said he thought he'd fumbled it too, so we shook hands again then launched into a long natter about all the bad handshakes we'd had, building rapport on the way and buying into each other's brand.

Tip #6 – Practice

The only way to really know how good a handshake you have is to find someone who will critique it. I do this all the time for my clients and they're often surprised that it's softer/harder/limper than they'd thought (yes, I'm talking about their handshake… keep it clean!) Ask someone to check for the overall feel, the pressure of the grip and the subliminal messages they're getting. Then, if your handshake needs a bit of work, practice. The more you do, the more natural your response will be when someone offers up their hand.

MWAH! AIR KISSING ETIQUETTE

For all that I know about personal branding, there's one area that has me stumped like an Ikea flat-pack: the air kiss. It's crept into British life and for many has become the norm for business greetings...but not everyone. That's when the trouble starts because a mismatch of approaches is a recipe for embarrassment. If I have my way, when I meet someone we'll smile, shake hands and say our names – simple. After all, we're business contacts, not family or friends (and certainly not bed-fellows) so that level of bodily contact seems appropriate.

Sometimes though, the person I'm meeting has other ideas. As I'm offering my hand, they're puckering up and heading for an air kiss. My brain thinks 'Whoa…wasn't expecting that!' closely followed by 'Quick…turn your head or they'll get you on the mouth!' closely followed by 'Which way? Are they going right or left?' And all of a sudden what was meant to be a confident interaction has left me fumbling around, mumbling my name into their ear as our cheeks touch and feeling generally off-balance. You can imagine my horror when the person decides to skip even that and begins extending their arms ready for a full bear-hug when we've only just met. (If I wanted a grope from a stranger I'd have taken the Tube.)

I've asked a number of people for their views and it seems they're as in the dark as I am. One person said that in France there are very clear rules: you meet someone, you kiss them three times and you repeat this each and every time you meet (although I can imagine a huge drawback if you're in the supermarket and keep bumping into the same person up and down the aisles).

Until we come up with such a black and white formula in the UK, I'll stick with a little strategy I've developed for those occasions where I'm totally at sea. It fits well with my personal brand for straight talking as I simply ask the person, "So what are we going for: a handshake, a kiss or a hug?" I make a note of the response and use that as my benchmark for subsequent meetings, although things can change over time and even I hug one or two of my contacts (just don't tell my sister - she only gets a peck on the cheek).

Some Dos and Don'ts about Handshakes

- **DON'T** ignore your handshake – it's a critical part of people's first impression of you.
- **DO** shake hands like you mean it.
- **DO** have the firmness of your hold reflecting the characteristics of your brand.
- **DO** maintain eye contact while shaking hands and **DON'T** forget to add a beaming smile.
- **DON'T** be afraid to flag up a bad handshake if it could give the wrong impression.
- **DON'T** ask me about the etiquette of air kisses – it's a mystery to me!

NAMES

"Knock, knock."
"Who's there?"
"Jennifer."
"Jennifer who?"
"Don't say you've forgotten me already!"

It's a small thing that can make a big difference to someone buying your personal brand: remembering their name. Doing so shows you value the relationship and that creates a very positive impression. And not doing so often has the opposite effect.

Here's what I'm talking about...

A client of mine called Susan says the moment someone calls her Sue she instantly takes a dislike to them. On occasion, she's even been known to say, "If I'd wanted you to call me Sue, I'd have introduced myself as Sue." Needless to say, they don't do it again.

Whenever I ask, "How good are you at remembering names?" the answers range from "Awful" to "Terrible" to "I've never been able to do it." Which is a lie, isn't it? Of course you can remember people's names (you know what to call your other half/kids/boss/ clients don't you?) What you might not be as good at is recalling the names of those you don't meet so often. That doesn't mean you can't get better at it though, so here are some more top tips.

REMEMBER, REMEMBER

Tip #1 – If you can, you will

The funny thing about your brain is that it tends to do what you tell it, even if it knows that's not necessarily what you want it to do. When you say, "I'm bad at remembering names," your brain colludes with you to prove you right. My first tip is therefore to

CUT IT OUT! Start telling yourself you're good at remembering names and your brain will come along for the ride.

Tip #2 – Put it front of mind

If you know you're facing a situation where you'll be meeting new people and need to remember their names, consciously tell yourself that's what you need to do. Turning up in a rush, thinking about the meeting you've just left and the emails stacking up in your inbox leaves little space in your noggin for taking on board something else, so make space by switching on your brain before you walk in the door.

Tip #3 – Repetition, repetition, repetition

The more chances you give your brain to hear someone's name, the better your odds of remembering it, so repetition is a good place to start. When they say, "Hi, I'm Claire," replying, "Nice to meet you Claire," gets you some scores on the doors.

If you want to go for the bonus ball, you could also say, "How do you spell Claire – with or without an 'i'?" It doesn't really matter, you're just chatting, but you've now heard their name three times and by asking a specific question you've switched on your brain that bit more and given it extra time to process what it's hearing.

Alternatively, if it's an unusual name, say, "Could you repeat that? I want to make sure I pronounce it correctly." They'll say their name again, you get another chance to repeat it and by now you've pretty much hit the repetition jackpot.

Tip #4 – Make it visual

A lot of people learn by seeing things written down and if you're one of those saying, "Do you have a business card?" should be your next move. You then read the person's name, look at their face and then back to the card to cement it in your mind's eye.

Tip #5 – Word association

Something that's useful for remembering someone's name longer-term is word association – linking a picture or phrase in your mind with the person standing in front of you. When you next meet them, you simply conjure up the association and use it to lead you back to their name. It's not without its pitfalls though: you need to ensure you say their name and not the association!

Here's what I'm talking about...
I can still recall a CEO named John Parker whose name I remembered by associating him with Parker from *Thunderbirds*. Or my client's receptionist called Lydia who I remembered with an old knock, knock joke the punch line of which was 'Lydia Dustbin'. Or a man with the surname Hunt that I remembered with a bit of rhyming slang (unrepeatable here, but memorable nonetheless!)

Tip #6 – Admit when you're stumped

Unless you're a savant with the ability to remember everything (think Dustin Hoffman in *Rain Man*) there will be times when a name just won't lodge in your brain. Perhaps it's because you didn't hear it in the first place, in which case it's perfectly OK to say, "I'm sorry, I didn't catch your name." Or perhaps it's because you're having another of your 'senior moments'.

Rather than doing that trick where you have a conversation in such a way that you avoid using their name (possible, but pretty stilted) why not say, "I'm sorry but your name has completely slipped my mind"? You could even make a joke of it in a way that's likely to illicit empathy from the other person – and even an admittance of the same – turning a negative into a great piece of rapport building.

Some Dos and Don'ts about Names

- **DO** make an effort to remember someone's name – it shows you value the relationship.
- **DON'T** tell yourself you're bad at remembering names – your brain will prove you right.
- **DO** find ways to repeat the person's name to cement it in your mind.
- **DO** use visual or word association prompts to help stick a name in your brain.
- **DON'T** avoid saying someone's name but **DO** admit if you've forgotten it.

"AND WHAT DO YOU DO?"

No matter whom I've worked with – from CEOs of large companies to entrepreneurs setting up their business – I've rarely come across anyone who relishes being asked, "And what do you do?"

Some tell me it's because they do so many different things they can't quite put it in words so end up saying, "Oh, you know, this and that." Hmm, this and that eh? Sounds a bit dodgy to me. Some say they feel embarrassed that they don't do something glamorous or interesting ("Me, oh I'm just a boring accountant"). Some tell me their job isn't something people have heard of or is just too complex to explain ("I'm a waste containment and environmental disposal specialist" – jargon for a bin man). And some tell me the reason they hate being asked is that they think saying their job title – "I'm a Chief Executive" – makes them sound like a big-headed bragger.

Any of those describe how you feel?

YOUR ELEVATOR PITCH

Dreading the question won't stop it being asked, so the smart thing to do is spend some time coming up with an answer that is so engaging the person you're talking to will want to know more. That's why I've created this little exercise to help.

WHAT TO DO: Set out the answers

Depending on when and where you're asked "And what do you do?" there are different points to cover, so get yourself a pen and paper and write down your answer to these questions. Remember…you're eventually going to have to say these, so brevity should be the order of the day – an absolute maximum of six or seven words for each:

Q1: What job do you do?
Q2: Who do you help?
Q3: What benefits do you deliver?
Q4: What do you do to deliver them?
Q5: Why is that important?
Q6: What are some great examples of when you've delivered?

WHAT TO DO: Put it all together

Now use the following formulae to put your answers together depending on your scenario.

Start with a short, snappy answer

"I help [Q2 answer] to [Q3 answer] because I'm a [Q1 answer]."

So the accountant from before might say, "I help SMEs to balance their books because I'm an accountant." That's very different from how we've been taught to give our answer (defining ourselves solely by our job title and the company we work for) so it may feel a little odd.

However, the reason you're placing how and who you help first and your job title second is because as soon as you tell someone your occupation their mind puts you in a box with everyone else they've ever met who does that job. That may not be too flattering (especially if you're lumped in with the boring accountants) so it's better to get them interested in the benefits you bring before revealing what you do.

Or better still, leave out the job title altogether:

"I help [Q2 answer] to [Q3 answer] by [Q4 answer]."

For example, a client whose original reply had consisted of a job title so convoluted it was mind-boggling ended up with the much better, "I help shareholders to buy and sell businesses by giving them the advice they need." You could even try being a bit more radical and deliver a message that really gets them thinking:

"I [mix of Q2 and Q3 answers]."

A client who's an auditor says, "I keep business people out of jail," then stops...says no more...not a word...and waits for the other person to enquire further.

Here's what I'm talking about...

As part of a workshop I was running I asked a woman, "And what do you do?" to which she replied, "I'm a tax consultant." I admitted that meant nothing to me, so I asked what she actually did. She replied, "I save people money." Now I was interested! Then I asked how she did that differently from other tax consultants. She replied with a twinkle in her eye, "I like to win," then shared some feedback she'd had from clients to that effect. We worked on the wording and came up with a new reply: "I save people money because I'm a tax consultant who likes to win. In fact, my clients say I'm like a like a dog with a bone if there's a way to pay less VAT." A couple of months later I bumped into her and she told me that, even though it had felt odd at first, she'd been using the response and had a great reaction. "People usually ask further questions, so they open the door to me telling them even more about the benefits I deliver." And she never feared being asked, "And what do you do?" again.

Add in a bit of 'how'

If you've got the person's attention, particularly with that last little tease, you'll likely be asked, "How do you do that?" If you haven't used it already, you could go the straightforward route:

"I do that by [Q4 answer]."

Unless it looks like you're in for the long-haul, remember to keep it short – they don't need to know the minute details of your working day. Using the previous example, the auditor adds, "I do that by making sure the numbers add up when I carry out an audit." If the person looks particularly interested, adding a bit of context to make it relevant to them can boost your answer further:

"There's a need for [Q5 answer] so I [Q4 answer] to do just that."

So the auditor might say the fuller answer, "Well, with more and more companies being put in the media spotlight, CEOs need to be sure their accounts are whiter than white. So I make sure the numbers add up when I carry out an audit."

Now's a good time to add a dash of personal brand too, using the magic word 'because' that you learnt on page 120. So the auditor makes sure the numbers add up "…because I can spot a dodgy figure from 50 paces" (promoting their Skill) or "…because I believe honesty is the only way to run a business" (promoting a Value).

Back it up with examples

By now you'll have them hooked like a sprat on a line, so it's time to give the listener something extra to identify with – a brief case study:

"One way I did that was [Q6 answer]."
Or "One time I [Q6 answer]."

Note I said 'brief' case study; keep it short and sweet and focus on illustrating the benefits you've already highlighted. I'll sometimes tell people, "One client I worked with had just taken over as MD and was due to give a speech at the annual sales conference. He planned to focus entirely on his strategy for the business, but I told him his staff needed to know who he was before they'd listen to what he had to say. We worked on his brand and he ended up beginning his talk with some some slides showing him as a professional footballer back in the '80s, complete with a mullet haircut, to explain his approach to leadership. I called his PA the next day to find out how it had gone and she said they'd really appreciated the personal background and felt more connected to him as the new boss." The key points are covered but it's taken me less than 20 seconds to say them.

IT'S BETTER FOR A METAPHOR

Sometimes, the quickest way to tell people what you do and how you do it is to give people a metaphor – a single clue from which the reference library in their brain can extrapolate a profusion of information. Plus, when it comes to ensuring you're talking in 9½mph language, a simple but effective analogy usually fits the bill.

Here's what I'm talking about...

Helen is a client who works as a compliance specialist for a large insurer, analysing operational situations and providing guidance on how best to resolve customer issues with particular regard to the management of risk. (Sounds riveting, doesn't it?) And while it might seem like an impossible task to make that sound interesting, she does it with aplomb. When asked what she does she replies, "People say I'm like a fairy godmother because I want a happy ending for everyone – the customer gets their problem fixed and the company gets its risk reduced." Didn't expect that, did you?

GIVE IT A WHIRL

Now you have your answer, go out and try it, tweaking it along the way as you learn what trips off the tongue and what doesn't. I guarantee you'll feel like a numpty the first time you do (I certainly did when I started telling people "I'm the double espresso of personal brand") but watch and listen to their response. They won't sneer and walk off in the other direction – unless they're devoid of a courtesy gene. On the contrary, they're likely to ask you more questions about what you do, which is exactly what you want, because now you can elaborate and promote your personal brand with impunity.

Some Dos and Don'ts about "And What Do You Do?"

- **DO** accept you're going to be asked, "And what do you do?" again and again, so you might as well spend some time crafting a good answer.
- **DON'T** start your answer with your job title.
- **DO** sell the benefits of what you do.
- **DO** plan different layers of response, depending on the time and place you're giving your reply.
- **DO** consider using a metaphor.
- **DO** try your answer out and keep tweaking it until it feels comfortable but **DON'T** think you'll feel anything other than a numpty the first time you try.

BUSINESS CARDS

You've gone to an event and avoided the pitfalls of making a bad impression so you think you're home and dry. But wait...they just asked for your business card: that little rectangle that says more about your personal brand than you might imagine – and which carries on saying it long after you've left the room. So get one of your cards out now. Go on, I'll wait for you...

Now you're back, take a good, long look at your card, read the wording, look at the logo, turn it over, feel the card, give it a bit of a flick with your thumb. While you're doing that, ask yourself this:

**I know what my personal brand is,
but does this card communicate that?**

IT'S MORE THAN A PIECE OF CARD

If your answer was "No" here are a few ways to get it back on track:

Size and shape

There's a standard size for UK business cards (85 x 55mm) and it's good to stick to that so your card will fit into people's filing systems, wallets, etc. If your brand is more stand-out though you can play around with the sizing but don't go too far off the mark. Too small and it will get lost, too big and it will end up in a different place from all the others (it's round and looks like a bin). Changes to the shape are an option too: rounded corners, cut outs and folding all help make it a little bit different.

Card weight

A flimsy card conveys a cheap brand and unless you're selling a product or service based on low price, steer clear of anything less than 300gsm thickness (your printer can help). Dirt cheap deals offered by online printers are rarely worth it when you consider the business you might be losing, because if you can't be bothered to invest in your brand, why should anyone else? (Remember Colin who handed me his disappointment along with his business card?)

Quality of print

As with the card weight, it's worth paying for decent printing to get the crispness of text and depth of colour to bring your card to life. If your ink's smudged or blurred around the edges, people will think that about your brand too.

Colours

There's a whole psychology to what different colours mean so think about what you want to say. Green is the colour of nature and suggests health, serenity, freshness and safety. Black is the colour of authority, power and sophistication. Blue is cool, calming and spiritual. Orange is the colour that stimulates enthusiasm and energy, vitality and endurance. Red is associated with fiery heat and warmth, though it can also mean danger.

Here's what I'm talking about...
I was once offered a choice of business cards by a contact. They all had the same information but came in different colours. After I'd selected a card, he told me what characteristics went with people who liked that colour. It made for an interesting start to the conversation.

Typeface

Just as with your emails and letters, the font you choose to have on your business card can also be used by the recipient to pick up clues. Go for one that has the same feel about it as your overall brand.

Content

When you think of the purpose of a business card, what's written on it is the important bit. Your card has to contain everything the recipient needs to know once you've parted ways: your name, what you do and how to get in touch, including Twitter, LinkedIn and Facebook if appropriate.

That may seem simple but I've had some cards where the person's just put their initial and not their full name, or there's only their company name and nothing to tell you what they do, or their phone number has been missing. I've ended up with the impression their attention to detail and understanding of my needs were somewhat lacking – not things I'm buying into.

Something that works well, if done with an eye firmly on quality, is to include a photo, making it even easier for people to remember who they were talking to.

Novelty

If you really want something 9½mph, how about handing over a business card that makes people say "Blimey!"

Like the owner of a delicatessen whose card is a miniature cheese grater. Or the survival expert whose details are printed on a piece of beef jerky (the sort adventurers tuck in their backpacks). Or the yoga instructor who hands over a tiny yoga mat that unrolls to reveal her name and number. Or the make-up artist who puckers up and puts a lipstick kiss on a card with her number already printed on it.

And for anyone who's thinking 'But I have a corporate business card and no say in how it looks' it's still possible to stand out from the crowd and be memorable:

- You could underline your mobile number with the words, "And here's the best number to get me on so I can speak to you personally," conveying the fact you value your relationships.
- You could write a personal note on it before you hand it over, something that has relevance to your conversation – perhaps the name of a restaurant you've recommended or a useful website – conveying a mutual interest and emotional connection.
- Or you can say something memorable when presenting your card. I was once given a particularly thick card with the words, "And it doubles up as an ice scraper." I'm never going to forget him!

WHEN IS A CARD NOT A CARD?

Much as I'm a fan of using your business card to convey clues to your brand, I'm fully aware that for many, they're a thing of the past. Nowadays, the mobile-savvy literally bump their phones together to exchange contact information, which in itself, still gives clues to your brand. (Namely, that you're a lot further ahead of the technology curve than me.)

Some Dos and Don'ts about Business Cards

- **DO** have a business card that carries on portraying your brand in a positive way, even when you're no longer in the room.
- **DON'T** waste money on cheap cards – they portray a cheap brand.
- **DO** consider the clues your choice of size, colour and typeface say about your brand.
- **DO** make sure the recipient has all the information they need to get in touch with you.
- **DON'T** think having a corporate card stops you from standing out from the crowd and **DO** hand it over in a memorable way.

SMALL TALK

Think of the times you've been at an event and started chatting to someone about business and, whilst the conversation was OK, it certainly wasn't riveting. Then think of the times when a bit of personal information popped into the conversation – maybe the person mentioned they'd spent the weekend rock climbing or were going to a gig to see their favourite band. All of a sudden, the conversation came to life and you started to enjoy the other person's company and, ultimately, their personal brand.

It was those relationship hooks (first mentioned on page 69) that did the job. They're the key to small talk: making it personal and, more importantly, being quick to do so. By getting your brand out there from the start, you can take months off the time it takes to get buy-in...and that's not so hard to do.

Here's what I'm talking about...

As the person in charge of partnerships for a financial organisation, Jacqui knew the importance of good relationships. I asked her how long those relationships took to get from 'business' to 'personal' and she reckoned about three months. She gave me an example of a guy she'd known for ages but it was only recently, when they'd been discussing holidays, that they'd discovered a shared love of skiing. We talked about how to get future conversations to the same point without the wait and here's what we came up with: when Jacqui meets people for the first or second time she's often asked, "How are you?" (A pretty standard question, you'll agree.) She replies, "I'm really well thanks, though I can't wait for my next holiday," which inevitably leads to her being asked, "Where are you off to?" and the answer is... skiing! It doesn't matter if it's a while before she'll be hitting the slopes, it's absolutely true. If the person she's met is also a skier, they'll go off-piste from the normal pleasantries, creating rapport on the way. Even if they're not a fan of the sport, it gives her a chance to ask, "What sort of holiday do you like?" and they're off again.

Another way to deliver relationship hooks is to include them in the visual clues you give about your brand. It might be having a photo of your dog as your screensaver so that other dog-lovers can pick up on it. It might be arriving at a meeting suited and booted but with a motorcycle helmet under your arm so that fellow bikers can pick up on it. It might be having a pair of cufflinks shaped like a boat so that fellow sailors can pick up on it. And even if the other person isn't into what you're into, it can still provide great fodder for an interesting conversation.

Here's what I'm talking about...
On meeting Alison for the first time I commented, "I like your scarf." It had zebras on it and she replied, "Thanks – I'm a fan of wildlife." I said, "Oh really?" and she said, "Yes, I even go on photography trips to see animals in the wild. The last time was to Alaska where I took photos of grizzly bears." My reply? "Wow!"

QUESTION TIME

Of course, small talk isn't all about the talking – you've got to listen to people too and asking questions helps you do that.

Even if you have nothing in common and know zilch about a subject, you can still show an interest in what interests them. So if they're a huge Man United fan and you wouldn't know Wayne Rooney if he stood up in your soup, all is not lost. Without knowing more than the absolute basics about football (it involves a foot and a ball) you can ask them:

- So why Man United?
- Do you have a season ticket?
- Do you go to many away matches?
- How different is it from watching the team play at home?
- How are they doing in the league this year?
- Who's their best player at the moment?

- Who's their best player of all time?
- How long have you been a fan?
- What's changed over the years?
- What do you love about the club?
- Are your family fans too?
- Am I asking too many questions???

TRY A DIFFERENT TACK

If someone has yet to throw you a bone when it comes to their interests the following questions may well help. They're from a blog by Gretchen Rubin, author of *The Happiness Project*, that was jam packed with juicy jabber gems to help the most daunted small-talker. Some were the old faithfuls like talking about the venue, the event, the food, the weather (and there's plenty of that in Blighty) or finding something newsworthy to comment on. Some were a bit more inventive though and my favourites were:

Ask a question that people can answer as they please, such as, "What's keeping you busy these days?"

As Gretchen pointed out, it's useful because it allows people to choose their focus – work, family, hobby – and extra helpful if you can't remember what the person does for a living. (Though if the occasion is a night on the town and the person you're talking to is dressed in a uniform with a hi-viz vest and handcuffs, it's probably better to keep schtum.) My own version of this has been, "So what's the biggest thing on your radar at the moment?"

Ask a follow-up question

Gretchen's example was asking, "Where are you from?" then following the person's answer with, "What would your life be like if you still lived there?" (My answer to the first question would be, "I grew up in Kent but I live in Yorkshire now," and my second,

"It'd be a bloomin' long commute.") As another example: building on the question I ask about what's on people's radars, I often follow up with, "What's your biggest headache with that?"

Ask getting-to-know-you questions

Gretchen's suggestions are, "What internet sites do you visit regularly?" or, "What holiday spot would you recommend?" as they often reveal a hidden passion, which can make for great conversation. (Though it's probably unwise to use the former when talking to an MP after statistics showed over 300,000 attempts were made to access 'adult' sites from Parliament.) I find, "If you had an unexpected day off, how would you choose to spend it?" can do the same thing.

Whichever route you choose, making small talk is a lot easier than you may give yourself credit for. Anyone can do it if you take an interest in the other person and give them the opportunity to take an interest in you. (And telling yourself you're rubbish at it will only perpetuate your brain's desire to prove you right.)

Some Dos and Don'ts about Small Talk

- **DO** get your small talk onto a personal, rather than business, level as quickly as possible.
- **DO** drop in some relationship hooks and look out for those of the other person.
- **DON'T** just talk...listen.
- **DO** ask questions.

ALCOHOL

While you're chatting away at an event, nattering about Andy Murray's latest win/defeat and who's done a show-stopping Tango on *Strictly Come Dancing*, it's very likely you'll have a glass in your hand. Depending on the time of day, it's also possible it will have alcohol in it.

There's nothing wrong with that – I'd be the last one to say abstinence should be the cornerstone of your brand. Where alcohol can be bad for you though is when it becomes your brand – remember that journalist I mentioned on page 48? I say 'can' rather than 'will' because sometimes it depends on your working environment.

Here's what I'm talking about...
I was running a workshop in Dublin and recounted the tale of the journalist whose brand was encapsulated in the phrase "That girl can drink!" Whilst the delegates understood the point I was getting across, one guy noted, in Ireland at least, that was actually quite a good brand to have and blokes with similar reputations were held in high regard (that is until full-blown alcoholism stopped them doing their job).

THE MORNING AFTER THE NIGHT BEFORE

The way I see it, when it comes to getting bladdered, you don't want to be the person everyone is talking about round the water cooler the next morning. Like the lad I worked with who was found unconscious by his front door because he'd drunk so much he couldn't get in and ended up in hospital with hypothermia. Or his team-mate who was taken out on a corporate jolly by a supplier and ended up dropping his trousers in the restaurant and getting everyone barred. Or the manager who picked a fight with another guy at the Christmas party and ended up falling down a flight of stairs. Or the executive who had to be put to bed by his colleagues because he was incapable of doing it himself, emerging the next day with a black eye he'd mysteriously sustained in his room. It's not just blokes who succumb to acting like imbeciles though – I've seen women just as trashed.

The fact I'm recounting these tales years after the event shows their ability to stick in people's minds – for all the wrong reasons. Even if it's a one-off occasion, it can blot your copy book. Keep it up and you'll end up with a stain on your reputation as impossible to shift as biro from your favourite shirt...even if you go teetotal.

So here's a bit of advice I was given by a PR sage when I first joined the sector, though it's relevant whatever job you do: always stay one drink behind everyone else. And after my own time wining and dining journalists I'd add: alternate every glass of booze with a glass of water and if you're meeting someone who has yet to buy into your brand, play it safe and take your lead from them; if they're drinking, have a drink, if they're not, don't. It'll save you an awful lot of hard work clawing back your good character further down the line.

Some Dos and Don'ts about Alcohol

- **DON'T** drink to excess – it's one of the quickest ways to ruin your brand.
- **DO** stay one drink behind everyone else and alternate every glass of booze with a glass of water.
- **DO** take your lead from the person you're with – especially if you've got a fledgling relationship.

STAYING IN TOUCH

As I mentioned before, people have to experience an advertising message a fair few times before it sinks in. Promoting your brand works the same way, so the more you can get on someone's radar (and stay there) the more likely that person will have you in mind when an opportunity arises – a promotion, a new job, a huge contract, a prospective client, a useful contact.

However, once you've called someone for the first time (chalk up one on the board), met them for a coffee (two), emailed to say you enjoyed the meeting (three) and perhaps dropped them a line a month later (four), you might find you run out of steam. Finding ways to stay in touch, that are relevant and personal, can help bump up the numbers.

THE A LISTERS

I'm not proposing you become pen pals with every person you meet (heck, I only call my mother once a week). What is a good idea though is to trawl through your list of contacts thinking about who it would be beneficial – for you and them – to have a strong relationship with. Those are your A Listers, the people worth investing a little time in (even going so far as to put reminders in your diary to keep in touch). And it really shouldn't take much time, because if you're canny you'll use every tool at your disposal.

GET SOME AMMO

I know from personal experience that getting in touch with someone is a lot easier if you have a reason to do so, otherwise you feel you're bothering them with a spurious "Hello" (it's not true of course, but that's how it feels). The trick is to find relevant things to mention – and there are plenty of ways to do that:

Follow their online updates

If you want to know what your A Listers are up to, why not get it from the horse's mouth? Follow them on Twitter, look for their updates on LinkedIn, even read their wall on Facebook. You can then do a number of things that will put you on their radars once more: drop them an email saying you'd seen their latest news, add a comment to their update, retweet their message with a few words of your own...things that take only seconds to do. Remember to add a personal touch though; it's OK to 'like' someone's update, but you'll build rapport better if you engage with them properly.

Set up alerts

Of course, there might be other things that are important to your A Listers that you're less aware of – business deals, annual results, sector news. Setting up Google alerts for any news that appears puts your finger on the pulse and could provide you with a reason for getting in touch. (Just Google 'Google alerts' to find out how.)

Here's what I'm talking about...

One of my former clients works for a well-known consumer brand that had received coverage in the trade press for a merger that was going on (something I'd never have normally seen but that was flagged by an alert). As we hadn't been in touch in a while I dropped him a note to see how he was faring. He was impressed I'd heard about the merger, touched that I'd thought of him and suggested we meet for coffee (giving me another chance to stay in touch).

Make notes

If you've paid attention to the section on Small Talk, it won't just be business you're discussing with your A Listers but personal stuff too. That can be a gold mine so jot things down (not then and there obviously but soon afterwards) and keep them somewhere handy, such as the notes section of their contact details. Some will be useful for adding to the conversation when you next meet, like remembering their kid's name, but others can be used more readily.

Here's what I'm talking about...
A PR consultant I know makes a note of what interests the various journalists she speaks to and keeps that in mind whenever she's reading any blogs or online articles. As soon as she comes across something relevant, she'll copy the link and drop the person a quick email saying she thought they might find it of interest. It's a really personal touch – and another bit of contact to add to the score!

Put a date in the diary

Listen out for details of any important dates coming up for your A Listers – they're giving a speech at the company's annual conference, or they're doing The Great North Run dressed as a gorilla. Then put a reminder in your diary for when it's happening and either wish them luck shortly before or find out how it went shortly afterwards. They'll be flattered you remembered and it'll open up a whole new avenue of conversation.

Ask for their help

Another way people feel flattered is when they're given the chance to share their knowledge. So if you have a problem that one of your A Listers might be able to help with, why not ask?

It could be as simple as seeking a recommendation for a venue near their office, or as complex as getting detailed background on their sector. In my experience, if you've already built a strong relationship, people are happy to let you pick their brains. Better still is when you follow that up with a quick note to say how their advice solved your problem, along with a big, fat "Thank you".

Provide expert information

Adding value is a great way to strengthen any relationship and provides another reason to stay in touch. Think about what would make your A Listers even better at their jobs, then deliver the goods. You might email them a link to a new piece of research, flag a useful website, tell them about an upcoming event or even provide your own expert advice via your blog.

Here's what I'm talking about...
I'd just emailed my A Listers with my latest blog about how to give your LinkedIn profile some pizzazz, when the phone rang. It was a client I hadn't spoken to in months who said, "Your blog was really timely as I've been meaning to sort out my profile for ages. It also reminded me that I wanted to talk to you about running some workshops for my staff, so let's have a chat about that now." Not only had my blog provided value, it got me some work to boot.

Drop by for a coffee

When it comes to staying in touch, seeing people in the flesh is the ultimate aim. Even if you just drop by for a quick "Hello" you'll have done a lot to refresh your brand in someone's mind. So whenever my work takes me to another city, I drop a line to my A Listers in the vicinity to see if they're free for a coffee. Even if they're not, we catch up via email and I'm back on their radar once more.

YOU DON'T ACTUALLY NEED A REASON

A contact of mine once sent me a newsletter that really hit a nerve. He said the reason businesses lose customers isn't because the person stopped liking them, it's because they lost touch. My mind instantly went to all the people I'd been meaning to ring/email/meet for a coffee and the guilt set in.

So I sat down and wrote a list of who they were and set about getting in touch, choosing three people every day to drop a line. Some I spoke to (it was lovely to hear how pleased they were I'd called), some I left a voicemail for (it still counted) and a few I emailed because I knew that was the best form of contact for them.

I didn't have a specific reason for any of them and it turned out it didn't matter. Just saying, "Hi, we haven't spoken in ages so I thought I'd see how you're doing – what's new with you?" was enough. It felt good because a) I'd made myself do something I could have easily avoided, b) I reconnected with lots of great people and c) it put us back on each other's radar. What could be simpler?

Some Dos and Don'ts about Staying in Touch

- **DON'T** lose touch – if people aren't reminded of your brand, their buy-in can turn to opt out.
- **DO** create a directory of A Listers who it would be mutually beneficial to stay in touch with.
- **DO** find reasons to get in touch by checking updates, setting up alerts, taking notes, putting dates in the diary, asking for help, providing expert information and dropping by.
- **DON'T** think you need a reason to get in touch – just saying "Hi" is fine.

PRESENTATIONS

Presentations are a great place to deliver a large dollop of your personal brand to a lot of people at once. It might be a formal affair, on stage with a microphone talking to a large gathering; it could be more select, with a few important people, some slides and cue cards; or it could be something casual, with just your team and a flipchart.

Wherever you are and whoever your audience, your brand matters from the get-go because the sooner you can get it across, the sooner they can buy into you. There are plenty of books out there to teach you how to hone your presenting skills, so let's focus on how to convey your personal brand while you're at it.

PLACING YOUR BRAND CENTRE STAGE

The thing to remember when you're on stage is that distance dilutes everything so you have to ramp up each aspect of your brand to the max. Even though you'll think you're being a bit dramatic, by the time your communication reaches the audience they'll think you're being normal. So here's how you go about it:

Your outfit

Remember that your Image is the packaging for your personal brand, so your outfit is the quickest way to give your audience clues – especially when all eyes will be on you. When you're presenting, those clues need to come across loud and clear and be picked up the second you take centre stage.

Whatever your Image, dial up to the top of your brandwidth and go for a stronger version of it – wear your sharpest suit, your brightest tie, your boldest jewellery, your highest heels and a little bit more make up. (Not all at once of course!)

Your sound

When you present don't think of it as anything less than you're putting on a performance. Just as actors use their vocal range to convey not just what's being said but the message behind it, so must you. This is all about dramatising what you're saying – longer pauses, wider tonal range, greater variance between loud and soft. Pretending you're Kenneth Brannagh might seem odd, but let me assure you, by the time your voice hits your audience's ears, it will have diminished to just the right level and represent your brand as it would be if you were speaking to each person one-to-one.

Your body language

Now you've increased your vocal range you need to make sure your body language matches, so don't forget to increase the drama in your gestures. One example is to act like the fisherman describing the one that got away: if you're opening your arms to illustrate something you're talking about, open them wider than you would normally. Again, the distance between you and your audience will temper the gesture back to its normal level.

> ### Here's what I'm talking about...
> I once worked on a presentation with an MD who didn't believe my advice to go a little over the top on the body language – until he saw a video of himself on stage. He'd resisted the big gestures because he thought he'd look like an eejit, but told me afterwards he wished he'd done them because he'd ended up looking bland instead of getting across his bold persona.

Don't forget to connect with your audience through eye contact too because looking directly at someone will strengthen the trust they have in your personal brand. Add a beaming smile to go with it to show you're genuinely enjoying your audience's company and you're onto a winner.

Your spoken language

We've already covered how positive language communicates a positive personal brand and it's just as imperative when you're presenting. It's amazing how many people apologise to their audience as soon as they take to the stage, whether it's, "Sorry the slides are a bit hard to read," or "Sorry if you can't hear me so well at the back." Of course, when the apology is done in a way that illicits a positive response, that's a different matter.

Here's what I'm talking about...
One executive I know who uses self-deprecation as a balance for his self-assurance took timidly to the stage with the line: "Sorry, I'm a bit nervous. This isn't the first time today I've got up from a warm seat with a piece of paper in my hand." He went on to be anything but nervous, knowing he'd raised a laugh and got the audience on side.

In addition to giving a flavour of your brand with your opening sentence, remember to pepper your presentation with some key words from your brand – hints as to your Values, Drivers, Reputation – using your new best friend 'because' (page 120 in case you've forgotten). And while you're at it, bung in a few relationship hooks too using stories and metaphors. They're a great way to bring a presentation to life so why not make them anecdotes about you?

Use that funny story about the time you locked yourself out of the hotel room on your honeymoon in just your underpants to illustrate risk management (whilst also letting them know your marital status plus somewhere you've been on holiday). Or relate the tale of how you once swam with sharks as a link to discussing your competitors' tactics (whilst sharing your love of diving and adventurous nature). I guarantee it will be these things that people come up and talk to you about at the end, because you've offered them a personal connection to your brand, not just a business one.

Here's what I'm talking about...

Back in my corporate days, the annual conference was an opportunity for the executive team to take to the stage. The presentation that sticks in my mind, despite the intervening years, was given by a director called Peter Craddock. He'd recently run the Marathon De Sables, a gruelling, multi-stage race covering over 150 miles in the Sahara, where temperatures can reach 50°C. As he told his story, Peter's point that you need to take any big challenge and break it down into smaller, manageable tasks came across loud and clear. But what really sticks in my mind is the tiny detail about how competitors would bandage each others' blisters each night (which he illustrated with a photo of his own battered feet), because it was so personal.

Your slides

Using slides as part of your presentation is a double-edged sword: great slides can be the cherry on your cake, giving a visual narrative to bolster the spoken one. But bad slides will detract from your words like a soggy bottom on what should be a tasty tart. So if you're going to use slides, be sure they're having the impact you want. A great book on the subject, and one that transformed my own slides, is *Presentation Zen* by Garr Reynolds. Its emphasis is on simple, uncluttered visuals that, with as little as a single image, provide a way to make your messages even more memorable.

Here's what I'm talking about...

A gentleman I know called Tony Ogden made sure his audience remembered his surname by using a picture of Stan and Hilda from *Coronation Street* on his opening slide. He then illustrated his messages about determination and resilience in business with a short video of triathlete Dick Hoyt and his disabled son Rick. (If you've not seen them before, check out YouTube.) Attendees said it left them feeling inspired, something that's now associated with his personal brand.

If you really want to get serious about putting your best foot forward when presenting, why not enlist the help of an expert? I've used Thor Holt (easily Googled with a name like that) to critique both my style and my slides before helping me to polish up both.

BE YOURSELF

Although you need to dial up your brand when you're presenting, be careful not to go too far – remember that outside your brandwidth there's only static. Be yourself by focusing on your brand pyramid and finding a natural presentation style to match. If you're an extrovert you'll likely find it easier, but even if you're an introvert you can still have presence in the spotlight.

One of the best presenters I've ever seen was my old boss, who would stroll back and forth across the stage, hands in his pockets, speaking slowly in a low tone, looking to all intents and purposes like he was talking to himself…but people were hanging off his every word. It's a far cry from the rabble rousing style of many CEOs, but just as effective.

Some Dos and Don'ts about Presentations

- **DO** all the things you'd normally do…just do them bigger, stronger and louder.
- **DO** get your personality out there quickly and **DON'T** just talk business.
- **DO** use stories and metaphors to bring your speech to life, especially if they offer your audience relationship hooks.
- **DO** use slides to add visual to your narrative, but only if they provide a cherry to your cake.
- **DON'T** be someone you're not – find a presenting style that matches your brand.

CVs AND INTERVIEWS

If there's one place you should feel entirely comfortable blowing your own trumpet it's in an interview…that's the whole point of it. The person sitting across the desk is asking you to sell yourself so they can make an informed decision whether they're buying what you have to offer. However, if you've been promoting your brand properly, you won't have waited until that exact minute to start; you'll have laid a trail of breadcrumbs to whet their appetite, both online and offline, one of which will be your CV.

YOUR VITAL STATISTICS

Your CV should be like a skirt: long enough to cover the basics, short enough to keep them interested, and what's included needs to count. So often though, people blether on about what they did, rather than what they achieved. Or worse still, they go to the other extreme and lay claim to things they didn't actually deliver – something that's gaining momentum with the younger generation.

Here's what I'm talking about…
According to an article in *The Sunday Times*, UK students are using *The Apprentice*-style bragging on their applications in order to bag a sought-after place at university. One teenager had seemingly climbed Everest as part of their schoolwork judging by their statement, "My achievements at school were vast." Another sounds like they would have given Gandhi a run for his money because, "I tackle the tasks presented to me with wisdom and sincerity." Better still though was the drama applicant who wrote that the first time they had been on stage was "inside my mother's womb." (I'm not sure there's an Oscar for Best Embryo yet, but give it time.)

To paraphrase an old advertising term, it's fine to sell the sizzle, but only if there's a juicy, appetising steak to go with it. A way to ensure that happens is to follow the advice of Janet Moran, founder of The CV House. When she's knocking her clients' career histories into shape, there are two questions she poses for every piece of information:

So what?
Says who?

In essence, what these questions do is make sure you really knuckle down to describing what you're bringing to the table, instead of using vague generalisations that make people wonder if you even know where the table is in the first place. The first question ensures you write about what you've delivered, not just what you did. And the second ensures you validate that rather than simply express your own opinion. To show how well the questions work, I'll give you an example of the sort of personal statement that adorns many a CV:

I am a highly accomplished [Says who?] *senior executive with an extensive track record* [Says who?] *of delivering major transformational change* [Says who?] *in a range of public sector organisations.* [So what?] *My innovative approach to leadership* [Says who?] *has enabled me to lead the way* [Says who?] *in combining a commercial approach with motivating my team.* [Says who? And so what?]

There's an art to getting it right and you can read how in countless books and blogs, so I won't cover the same ground. Where I'm coming from is the less obvious stuff that can give more clues to your brand than just what you've written – the stuff that if you can't get it right here, when can you get it right?

The primary one is spelling and grammar, because a mistake sends the message, "I can't even present myself in the best light so I'm probably not going to present your company in the best light either." It shouldn't be hard to nail, especially if you ask someone else to read it for you (assuming they have a decent grasp of English).

Here's what I'm talking about...
A recruiter I know was sounding off about the poor quality of
candidates' CVs, telling me about the person who'd been to
'grammer school' (oh the irony), the one who had worked in 'pubic
relations' and the person who'd listed their skills as: 'team player,
attention to detail, hard working, trustworthy, attention to detail'.
Doh!

A lot of the things that apply to letters (see page 111) apply here
too. Firstly, think about the font you use for your CV: different
typefaces convey different messages, from youth to gravitas. Then
think about the paper and envelope you print it on: go for quality
and try and keep it pristine, not like the one I once received with a
coffee stain on it (at least I hope it was coffee).

If you're filling in an application form or writing a covering letter,
consider your handwriting: if it's great, use it, at least for the
salutation and sign-off, but if it looks like a five-year-old's scrawl
try to stick to the keyboard.

And while you're at it, consider the pen you use: even the ink
colour reveals something and not always in a good way, as the
person who used a pink glitter pen to fill in a job application I
received was obviously unaware of.

Plus don't forget to check what your email address is saying –
grumpyoldgit@gmail.com is unlikely to go down well.

Even how you deliver your CV is worth a thought; dropping it off
in person means that first impression is made with the benefit of
your voice and body language – not just the written word. You
may not be able to see the person who's advertised the job, but
the receptionist will still have taken note of you and they carry a
lot more sway than you might think. (I know plenty of people who
ask front of house staff for their views on a candidate.)

COVER ALL THE BASES

It's not just your CV that could nab that interview; if one's been requested, your covering letter is just as important and is a great place to drop in those subtle brand clues. Choose a couple of key ingredients from your brand pyramid and weave them into what you write, using 'because' where necessary. Don't go overboard though; this isn't about replicating the whole thing word for word, as the prospect of wading through *War & Peace* will turn the reader off.

YOU'RE IN

Hooray! Your CV and letter were so compelling you got the interview. Now what are you going to do? If you're like most of the population, you'll start trying to figure out what questions you could be asked and how you're going to answer, spending time coming up with real-life examples and convincing statements. That's all good, especially if those answers include some specific clues to your brand – because people buy people, so it's your job to help them understand what they get from buying you.

Here's what I'm talking about...

Helen was a job-seeking exec who came to me after she got to final stage interview on two occasions but had been unsuccessful because, as one interviewer put it, "We knew you could do the job, but we didn't get any idea of you as a person." She'd been so good at selling the 'what she does' she'd omitted any of the 'who she is' – her personal brand. We worked on what Helen brought to the table along with her many skills and she now promotes the two in tandem for a more balanced view.

What you'll have likely overlooked is that your answers will count for nought if you haven't got the first impression right. Spend as much time preparing for the first few minutes of the interview as you spend on the rest and you'll increase your chances of acing it.

That means planning your journey so that you arrive at least half an hour in advance. This allows time for any delays and also to suss out where the front door is (I've been foxed by that a number of times). Don't walk into the reception straight away though; find a place to have a cup of tea then go back 10 minutes before your allotted appointment. That's enough time to show you're organised, but not so much that it'll cause the interviewer to panic because they're not ready.

It also means working out what you're going to wear that will make you feel confident (remember that enclothed cognition) and deliver specific clues to your brand. Plus make sure that as you dial up your Image you stay within your brandwidth.

For instance, if you feel that wearing a tie is the equivalent to putting a noose around your neck, don't wear one. If the only reason someone gives you the job is because of your neckwear, that's not a great fit with your brand and you won't enjoy working there. If, however, wearing a tie isn't something that bothers you, go ahead and put one on.

Practising your handshake will also be time well spent, especially if it's something the interviewer uses to get the measure of someone.

"FINE THANKS" IS NOT AN OPTION

You also want to work out some engaging answers for when you're greeted with, "How was your journey?" (please don't answer with a 10mph "Fine thanks") or "Did you have any trouble finding us?" (just "Yes" or "No" are not acceptable responses). Remember that it's those relationship hooks that build rapport quickly, so find a way to put them out there.

For example, if you're asked about your journey you could say, "The train took an hour but I was so engrossed in my book the time flew by." That'll likely illicit the question, "What are you reading?" Your answer may well be met with, "I've read that, it's good isn't it?" (and their brain's reference library will see it as a positive that you share the same taste in books). You may also get, "I've read that, but I didn't like it," or "I haven't read that." Either way, the conversation needn't stall as it's your cue to ask, "What books do you like to read?" and off you go again.

This is the stuff that matters just as much as your answers to the business questions. Because when the interview is over and you've left the room, they won't simply refer to you in their discussions as 'the guy who said he'd delivered a £3 million project', they'll also be saying 'the guy who reads the books'.

WHO'S BUYING WHO?

Before we leave the subject of interviews, I want to remind you once again of the biggest confidence booster you've got: accepting that not everyone will buy your brand. People buying people is a two-way street and if it ain't working for you, walk away, because the secret to being happy at work isn't finding someone else has removed the paper jam from the photocopier. It's this:

Working for a company whose Values match your own.

When you're the head honcho of the company, that's easier to achieve because you can change the culture to suit you. However, when you're further down the pecking order your hands are tied.

So it's important to get the match of Values right from the start – to seek an employer who has at the heart of their business the same moral compass that's leading you on your career journey. If, for example, your Values are that 'we're all created equal and fairness matters at all cost' you'd be well suited to working for a mutual like John Lewis or Nationwide. If that matters less to you than a Value to 'provide for my family at all costs' being an investment banker with Goldman Sachs or UBS shouldn't be a problem. I'm not saying one is better than the other, but I am saying that knowing exactly what your Values are and looking for those in your employer can make the difference between bouncing out of bed in the morning and dragging yourself into the office. Plus it's not just when you're looking for a new job that you should switch on your Values antenna.

Here's what I'm talking about...

I worked with one client who had been with the same company for over a decade. Although his role, the people he worked with and the activities he undertook hadn't substantially changed, he'd started to feel less engaged but couldn't understand why. Once we'd defined his personal brand, all became clear: his Values of being ethical, entrepreneurial and close to the customer, which had been a perfect fit in the early days of the business, had got lost in a larger company culture. The mismatch between his brand and the company's brand had crept in without him even realising.

I'm not a complete utopian though; in tough times when just having a job can be a blessing, there is often a trade-off to be made and only you can decide how far you're willing to flex your brand to keep your pay-cheque. But if you are at liberty to do so, put 'matching Values' on the top of your shopping list for a job and you'll have hit the jackpot.

Some Dos and Don'ts about CVs and Interviews

- **DO** ensure your CV is 100% accurate and **DO** get someone with a decent grasp of English to proof read it.
- **DON'T** just prepare for the questions you'll get mid-interview – **DO** think just as much about the first impression you'll make.
- **DON'T** forget it's a two-way street. You have to buy their brand as much as they have to buy yours and **DO** look for a clear match of Values.

PROMOTING YOUR BRAND: ONLINE

The advent of online communication has created a massive audience who could potentially buy your brand. What baffles me is how many people are resistant to putting themselves out there, using all manner of excuses from, "I don't like people knowing about me," to "I wouldn't know what to say about myself," to "I really can't be bothered." (At least they're brutally honest.)

I understand why people might prefer to keep to themselves and if you can exist without the need for people to buy you, I genuinely wish you well. However, most of us have to earn a crust and it's a lot easier to get a job/client/contract if people can find you than if you remain as elusive as the Scarlet Pimpernel. How will they do that? By looking online of course.

ONLINE BRANDING

A guy once said to me, "If I Google someone and nothing comes up about them, I assume they don't exist." It's a harsh and somewhat dismissive view, but in a lot of ways he's right – being online should be a basic of your brand, not an add-on.

Here's what I'm talking about...

When I was first due to meet Alan Halsall, I checked him out on Google and found virtually nothing. I'd expected more for the Chairman of Britain's leading pram-maker, Silver Cross, so when I met him I asked why he wasn't at least on LinkedIn. He replied he'd never seen the point (those who needed to know him already knew him) but as we spoke he started to understand the benefits. We ended up developing his online profile and a while later he flew to Hong Kong for the opening of the company's first store there. A

Chinese journalist who was covering the story introduced herself then added, "I've already Googled you so I know about your background." He'd travelled nearly 6,000 miles and, thanks to his online profile, those who needed to know him already knew him.

Once you've got your online brand up and running, there are plenty of free tools to help you work out how much of an impact it's having on the worldwide web. Check out ones like www.onlineidcalculator.com to rate your efforts and influence, while others like www.profiled.com or www.brandyourself.com (or even Google alerts) can flag when you get a new mention so you can keep tabs on yourself.

GOING VIRAL

That last point is important since, despite all you might be doing to peddle a positive reputation, there's little stopping someone else depicting you in a negative light. Sometimes that could be a disgruntled employee or an unhappy customer venting their spleen, but sometimes it could be of your own making.

Now, I recognise I'm making a statement of the bleeding obvious by saying you should never write something you'd be mortified if a) it appeared in the press and b) your mother would be so embarrassed she could never show her face in the corner shop again. However, judging by the amount of people who overlook that advice and end up red-faced, it's worth making the point.

Plus it's not just when a story is about you that it can have an effect. Simply having a connection to someone who has damaged their personal brand can put a dent in yours. People judge you by the company you keep, so the next time you accept an invitation on LinkedIn or write a recommendation, take a minute to ask yourself how sure you are of that person's credibility and reputation.

Here's what I'm talking about...

Kelly Blazek manages a list of marketing jobs in Ohio and received an invitation to connect on LinkedIn from a young jobseeker. Riled by the whippersnapper's alleged impertinence, she responded with a stern rebuke that lamented the "inappropriate" and "tacky" request. Commenting, "Wow, I cannot wait to let every 26-year-old jobseeker mine my top-tier marketing connections to help them land a job. Love the sense of entitlement in your generation," she ended by saying, "Don't ever write to me again." The reason we know this is because it went viral on Twitter, got picked up by the media in the US, then by the media worldwide. So you have to feel sorry for the members of the local business group who had previously awarded her Communicator of the Year!

If this happens to you, you need to know about it as soon as possible (hence setting up alerts) because once bad press starts floating around the ether, it's very hard to get rid of it. Unless you can bring in some legal guns to fight your corner, the only real ammunition you have is to keep pumping out positive mentions to try and push the negative stuff further down the search results.

CHOOSE YOUR CHANNEL

An online presence is important but you don't have to be all over the internet like a rash. Choose the channels most relevant to the people you want buying your brand and use those...but do it well. (A good book on the subject is *Jab, Jab, Jab, Right Hook* by Gary Vaynerchuk.)

You might be sitting there thinking, "Ha, got this one sussed, I've already got a LinkedIn profile and even send the odd tweet," but have you done any quality control to check how good the messages you're sending about your brand are? Have you had feedback on your profile or seen how many people retweet your musings? It's better to use one or two online channels effectively than three or four half-heartedly. We'll go into some specifics about LinkedIn,

Twitter and Facebook later but first let's cover some things that apply wherever you're touting yourself on t'internet.

ADD SOME PERSONALITY

Language becomes ultra-important when you go online. Without your physiology and tone of voice you have to work doubly hard to have a bit of personality. That means steering clear of the same business speak and clichéd language everybody else is using, or you'll end up as the big, fat 'me too' I mentioned on page 86.

To get an idea of how you're currently faring, let's play a quick game of Bad Buzzword Bingo, courtesy of LinkedIn's annual trawl of its users' profiles to find the 10 most overused words. These are the things that so many people are saying, everyone else has stopped listening. It's a global list but LinkedIn did note that 'enthusiastic' is in the top 10 only in Britain.

So get yourself a copy of your profile (from LinkedIn or elsewhere) and a red pen to circle any 'winning numbers' from the following:

1. Responsible	6. Expert
2. Strategic	7. Organisational
3. Creative	8. Driven
4. Effective	9. Innovative
5. Patient	10. Analytical

How did you do? It's not the end of the world if you had one or possibly two, but please tell me you didn't get a full house!

Interestingly, one that's not on there but is my personal bug-bear is the word 'passionate'. It's a great word but one that's become a staple of every talent and reality show wannabe ("I'm passionate about singing/acting/dancing/modelling/cooking/baking/sewing/hairdressing/gardening/whateverelseyoucanthinkof") so think twice before using it.

THE PERSON BEHIND THE KEYBOARD

Using engaging language that avoids the 'blah' is only part of the story. The other is making sure your online communication includes a bit of your personal brand (with the emphasis on the personal) because it's not just the 'what' that counts but the 'who' too. To show you what I mean, imagine you've gone onto a company's website and are reading the biographies of three of its executives:

Tom Smith – HR Director

As HR Director, Tom Smith has responsibility for the organisation's strategic policies on people management and the development of non-core training for next generational leaders. He is also the Chairman of the company's remuneration committee.

Tom has worked for Logitalk since 1990, starting in the recruitment team before moving to head the Learning & Development Division, where in 2006 he led a project to formalise the organisational structure of the Logitalk Group. This led to the company receiving a number of awards, including the gold standard from Investors in People.

Tom has experience in both public and private sectors and previous organisations include Barclays, HSBC and the NHS. He is also is a non-executive director of the Chamber of Commerce's subsidiary training company and a past president of the Association of HR People.

Richard Jones – Legal Director

As someone who believes strongly in the principles of fairness and justice, it's no surprise Richard Jones began his career as a lawyer. Starting in private practice, he moved into the not-for-profit field working for the charity Advantage, before returning to his roots as Logitalk's in-house solicitor.

For Richard, being professional means being prepared: doing his homework, gathering knowledge and listening to others in order to voice an informed opinion. He is also a strong communicator who engages with people at all levels and chooses his words to have the greatest impact.

Once called 'the glue that holds it all together', Richard's strong work ethic fits squarely with his belief that success should be measured on talent and ability, not status; a highlight of his career was winning the Legal Director of the Year Award in 2010.

Harriet Williams – Business Development Director

Like a lot of people in business, Harriet Williams gets immense enjoyment from hitting a target. Sometimes those are work targets, like selling an idea for a new income stream or setting up a company from scratch. Other times those are personal targets, like gaining an MBA whilst working full-time and bringing up children, or running the New York Marathon.

Harriet uses her abilities to see the big picture and spot income opportunities to develop projects for Logitalk which bring big commercial benefits. As a result, in 2013 income from partnerships increased by 38%.

Harriet's energy and tenacity to get the job done are mixed with a lot of fun, especially when she's enjoying her hobby of kayaking around the British coastline.

Now let me ask you a question:

Who will you remember in 24 hours' time?

If you're anything like the hundreds of people I've asked on my workshops, you'll have chosen Harriet (or at the very least Richard).

That's because Harriet put some 'person' in her profile, adding a human element to the words on the screen, so you get to know her even before you've met her. Now you need to do the same.

Some Dos and Don'ts about Online Branding

- **DO** brand yourself online – people will be Googling you and if they can't find you they might assume you don't exist.
- **DON'T** post anything you wouldn't be happy for your mother to read and **DO** be careful about the online company you keep.
- **DON'T** use every online channel going but **DO** choose one or two that best fit with your audience.
- **DON'T** be a 'me too' by using 10mph language, especially in your online profile.
- **DO** make more of an effort to use personal language as being online means you don't have the benefit of tone of voice or physiology to get your brand across.

ONLINE PROFILE

Your online profile is the best advertising space you have for your brand – so use it! Make sure your biography is ready for people to find and make sure they love it when they do. Even if you read those profiles earlier and can safely say yours is a long way from the dullness of Tom Smith's, if I could take your name off it, put someone else's on and not really know the difference it's not enough. (It's even worse if your online profile isn't even about you but the company you work for instead.)

Unless you can say, hand on heart, "There's nobody out there who has a profile like mine and it gives a great first impression of what people will get when they meet me," you have some work to do.

That's where I can help…

3 IS THE MAGIC NUMBER

I'm going to share a secret with you (with a little help from 80s hip hop group De La Soul): three is the magic number when it comes to creating an online biography to be proud of – be it for a website, LinkedIn or anywhere else. By including a blend of three key elements, weaving them into a story that holds the reader's attention (not just three individual chunks), you can get buy-in to who you are and what you have to offer without even being in the room.

Element #1 – Examples of your credibility

Traditionally, business profiles are written wholly with examples of credibility (see Tom Smith's on page 181). Whilst stating where you've worked, the positions you've held, who your clients have been, the qualifications you have and the results you've delivered are all good things, if that's all you have to say it ends up dull, dull, dull.

Instead, choose one or two facts that really show you at your best and leave the rest back on your CV. Aim for ones that have impact: the targets you met, the profits you increased, the awards you won, the clients you serviced, the business you created. To help pinpoint these, ask yourself:

Q: What am I proud of having achieved in my career?
Q: What's the best result I've got for a client?
Q: What hard facts quantify my success or credibility?
Q: How did I come to be doing what I do?
Q: What major projects am I working on right now?

Here's what I'm talking about...
Including credibility in your profile, especially if it involves some key words that are relevant to your sector, can work wonders for your career. A case in point is Tony Ogden (the guy from page 168) who updated his LinkedIn summary to put emphasis on his health and safety background. That brought him to the attention of a contact he'd not seen for over 20 years, who picked up the phone and headhunted Tony for a job.

Element #2 – Your personal brand

As well as telling people what you've achieved, the second element is to tell them which parts of your personal brand helped you achieve them. That gives readers a better understanding of what makes you tick (see Richard Jones' profile as an example).

Try to choose the aspects of your brand that link to your credibility examples so you can tie the two together, as in: 'Richard's strong work ethic fits squarely with his belief that success should be measured on talent and ability, not status' and 'a highlight of his career was winning the Legal Director of the Year Award in 2010'.

To help, ask yourself:

Q: What are my strongest personal brand traits?

Q: What do I deliver that others don't?

Q: Which aspects of my brand appeal most to my clients?

Q: What's the best part of my job and how does that fit with my brand?

Here's what I'm talking about...

After delivering a seminar on personal brand, I was approached by a man called Brian Canavan. His face looked familiar and he told me he'd attended the same event a year earlier when I'd also been the speaker. It turned out my comments at the time about the need to make your LinkedIn profile personal had struck a chord. He'd duly gone off and made changes and was soon experiencing some staggering results. As he said, "I had made the cardinal sin of reciting my 'what' as a list of skills in my profile summary with very little about the 'why'. I immediately changed my profile and within a week I had enquiries from people I'd never met but who found me on LinkedIn, asked to meet and ended up as new clients. I asked what was the deciding factor and in every case it was that my profile had resonated with them personally. They were all engaged by the fact that I stated the motivation for doing what I do and this fantastically simple change continues to lead to great results."

Element #3 – Relationship hooks

To add some personality to your words you should polish off your profile with a couple of relationship hooks – something that in one small clue speaks volumes about your personal brand and has the added bonus that when people meet you they can use it as a conversation starter. This can be anything people might find interesting about you. Try and choose things that will make you stand out and be memorable; saying you like to read in your spare time isn't nearly as interesting as saying you love crime fiction and collect first editions of Sherlock Holmes. To help, ask yourself:

Q: What do I do in my spare time?

Q: What unusual or interesting things have I done or have happened to me in the past?

Q: What would people be surprised to learn about me?

Aim to find ways to tie your relationship hooks together with the other elements, as in: 'Harriet's energy and tenacity to get the job done are mixed with a lot of fun, especially when she's enjoying her hobby of kayaking around the British coastline.' She's tied her personal brand with a relationship hook. Alternatively, she could have tied the hook with a piece of credibility by saying: '…like gaining her MBA whilst working full-time (and still finding time to kayak around the British coastline)'.

For anyone reading your profile in advance of meeting you, these are gems with which they'll be able to start a great conversation.

Here's what I'm talking about…

Anyone checking out my online profile quickly spots my relationship hooks: '*I balance being in the limelight by living my version of The Good Life in the Yorkshire Dales: pottering around the garden in my wellies, keeping bees and feeding chickens, then ending the day with a well-deserved glass of Rioja while listening to The Archers*'. You wouldn't believe how many people have introduced themselves to me saying, "I keep bees too!" or, "May I buy you a glass of wine?" (always a good question) and even, "So what do you think about the latest goings on at Bridge Farm?" (It turns out a lot more people listen to *The Archers* than you'd think.)

CHOOSE YOUR HOOKS WISELY

While we're on the subject, don't forget that any relationship hooks you're using need to sit 'above the line' and give positive clues to your brand (remember the ladder on page 67?) For instance, mentioning alcohol as I do is OK if you're well into your career or your own boss, but doing so when you're a graduate looking for your first job is a different matter. Things like stating which football team or political party you support should also be given some thought. I'm not saying you mustn't mention these things, only that you should think about how they might be received and perceived if you do.

HERE ARE SOME I MADE EARLIER...

To show you some real-life examples of the magic number in action, here are a few profiles I've written for my clients' websites and LinkedIn profiles. Some put more emphasis on one element than another (reflecting that person's brand and business priorities) but all give you a strong idea of who that person is in real-life:

Alan Halsall, Chairman, Silver Cross

For Alan Halsall, business isn't about making a quick buck – it's about investing time and energy for the long-term, focusing on the here and now in order to grow a company for the next generation.

Alan started his professional life following in his grandfather's footsteps as a qualified lawyer, but a hankering for something more exciting led him to join the family business in 1979. With his strategic direction and his brother's skill as a trader, Halsall's grew to become the UK's largest privately owned toy company, with a turnover of £72 million, before it was sold in 2006.

As a man who thrives on being busy, Alan was ready for the next challenge and hearing Silver Cross had gone into receivership acquired the company three days later. In his position as Chairman he has created teams of talented people who have helped him grow this iconic brand into the multi-million pound success story it is today.

With his infectious enthusiasm, Alan's biggest thrill comes when he's travelling the world and sees a new mother getting pleasure from pushing her baby in a Silver Cross pram. Back home, he indulges his passion for horseracing as the owner of some moderately successful winners. Fascinated by UK politics, Alan is also a member of the Carlton Club and has represented the voice of northern manufacturing on a number of Treasury groups.

Alasdair McGill, Co-Founder, LowerYourScores.com

I'm not a man to sit about – both figuratively and literally. As a company CEO and a keen sportsman, I believe in living life to the max, whether mind mapping an idea that's come to me in the wee small hours or hitting the gym before breakfast. But my excitement for what I do means neither feels like hard work.

I have a brain that is always busy and love thinking of creative ways to be disruptive, asking, "Why does it have to be that way?" with the ultimate aim of giving the customer a better experience. Throughout my career, I've been led by a strong belief in honesty and integrity (something instilled in me by my late father). I've twice had to make tough decisions to do the right thing after uncovering serious frauds, putting my principles before my personal situation. However, I believe that by staying true to your values you will always come out the other side – and so I have.

I learnt a lot from those experiences, just as I did when I broke my collarbone in a cycling accident in 2010. Out of action for over six weeks, I discovered my forte is spending time on the business, and less in it, using my creativity to keep challenging the status quo. Now back on the bike, I continue to ride most weekends, as well as the odd jaunt from London to Paris to raise money for charity, all the while enthusiastically blogging about my experiences.

Helen West OBE, Director, Kendal Blue

Every job in my career has been about one thing: maximising customer service – whether designing new approaches, developing teams, growing organisations, transforming performance, or restructuring to reduce costs.

I established and led two Business Link organisations, the largest of which provided services to over 120,000 businesses across Yorkshire and the Humber. Working for a private sector firm delivering public sector services, I transformed the company to a £35 million business, doubling output in a 12 month period and generating £35 for the local economy for every pound spent. In 2007, I was awarded an OBE for services to business.

Following cuts in public spending, my role focused on steering the company through successful downsizing and eventual closure, while keeping staff engaged and delivering services right through to the very last day. Indeed, we achieved our highest levels of customer satisfaction in our closing months.

Delivering against the odds is what I love, whether it's in work or my spare time (as a regular camper I'm known for never giving in, despite the weather) and can always find the positives to focus on.

Deri Llewellyn-Davies, CEO, Business Growth International

When it comes to Deri Llewellyn-Davies, the phrase 'suited and booted' takes on a new meaning. As the UK's leading authority on bringing strategy alive, Deri spends his days in a pinstriped three-piece and his spare time climbing the highest summits in the world (just one of his extreme exploits). Deri loves business and adventure in equal measure and his same motivation underpins both: a fascination with life and a curiosity that always leads him to ask "Why?" or more importantly "Why not?"

That questioning is key in his role as CEO of Business Growth International, as he helps leaders in both FTSE 500 and entrepreneurial companies to take their businesses (and themselves) to the next level. With over 15 years' experience of the commercial markets, Deri knows that whatever issues his clients are facing – from funding shortages to management fall-outs, redundancy to bankruptcy – he's been there and got the T-shirt. It's exactly that experience that fuels his ability to look at their business and connect the hidden dots, leading him and his clients to the heart of the issue.

Deri still makes time for his adventures though, and is part way through a self-styled 'Global Adventurer's Grand Slam' – something he created aged 30 when an injury sustained during an international tournament ended his rugby career. Having completed the Marathon des Sables and climbed five of the world's highest summits, Deri has only two more mountains, both Poles, an Iron Man and a jungle marathon to go.

HE, SHE OR I?

As you may have noticed from those examples, there are two ways you can write your profile: in the third person (he this, she that) and in the first person (I this, I that). The former tends to be used for company websites, although when the company comprises only one or two people the first person can work well too, as it's more intimate. However, according to LinkedIn expert Mark Williams from ETN Training, the accepted rule for the site's online profiles is to write in the first person as you're appearing as an individual – albeit you might work for a company. Saying 'I' makes it personal.

Another thing to consider is word count. LinkedIn sets a 2,000 character limit so your profile summary can only ever be a certain length but I suggest aiming for around 300 - 350 words to keep the reader engaged. With a company website you can afford to go a bit longer; anything up to 400 - 450 words is OK, so long as it's interesting. (You could of course bring your words to life by adding a video to your profile, either on your company website or LinkedIn.) And don't forget your headline too: simply including your job title is a wasted opportunity when you could be adding some 9½mph copy.

GET IT RIGHT (AND GET SOME HELP)

I'd like to end this section with a little bit of advice: I know from personal experience how hard it is to write your own profile so don't think this is going to be a walk in the park; it's going to take a bit of time to get it right, but it will be time well spent if people are buying your brand before they've even met you.

If you're not a natural writer, enlisting the help of someone else can be a godsend. It might be a paid professional (it's a service I offer, so feel free to get in touch) or a gifted friend, but whoever it is they could save you a lot of time and headache.

Once it's written, test your profile out on someone who knows you well to see if they feel it reflects your brand and does the justice you deserve. Or read it aloud to get a feel for how it will flow for the reader. And give it a final spell check before posting!

Some Dos and Don'ts about Online Profiles

- **DO** put your profile online – it's prime advertising space for your brand, so use it.
- **DON'T** have a profile that you could take your name off and put someone else's on and never know the difference.
- **DO** include three magic things in your profile: credibility, personal brand and relationship hooks.
- **DO** choose wisely which relationships hooks to include.
- **DON'T** use the third person on LinkedIn – **DO** write 'I'.
- **DO** check spelling and grammar before putting your profile online.

PROFILE PHOTO

Just as much as the written word that accompanies it, your profile photo is an opportunity to give people an idea of what you're all about. In fact, LinkedIn did a study to track where people's eyes go when they look at someone's profile and, after reading the person's name, the place they go to (and spend longest) is looking at the picture.

Having a photo is non-negotiable in terms of your personal brand. Even the excuse, "But I don't take a good picture" or, "I've got a wonky smile" won't sway that. Be sure to give it some thought beforehand though, because there are plenty of people who haven't. A quick look online will soon show you what I mean. Dodgy photos abound and as it's sometimes best to explain what not to do, here's list of things to avoid. (All of these examples are based on genuine profile photos I've seen whilst on LinkedIn.)

ROGUE'S GALLERY

The Bride

Everyone knows a lady never looks lovelier than on her wedding day, but using a shot of you with a tiara on your head or your hair in some fancy do is not representative of you at work – so why use it? (The same goes for guys: the buttonhole and cravat is not standard office wear.)

The Hobbyist

You may think I'm kidding with this one, but browsing LinkedIn one day I came across someone who had a photo of himself dressed as Elvis (pay me enough and I might just reveal who it is!) Whilst relationship hooks about what you do for a hobby can certainly give clues to your personal brand – in this case their taste in music and a certain sense of fun – which is good, it's best saved for Facebook or Twitter where 'business gravitas' isn't the order of the day.

The Tourist

When you're on holiday you tend to take more photos than you would normally, so there's a bigger selection to choose from...I get the logic. What I don't get though is the illogical thought that having a photo of you in a bikini on your business profile is perfectly acceptable. Plus the cocktail or beer in your hand may not be sending the messages you want.

The Loved One

This one's been creeping in recently – people who use snaps of them with their pet or child. It's all very cutesy, but not very business-like (is this Fido's profile or yours?) The worst I saw was someone who had used a photo of himself with his son on his shoulders, but he'd cropped it so that it looked like he had two arms and legs growing out of his head.

The Status Symbol

You've had your picture taken with a status symbol – a fast car or a yacht – and you've chosen it to say something about you (the insinuation being that it is yours and you're incredibly wealthy). Either way, by trying to include the item in the background, your face ends up so small in the photo people have no idea what you look like.

The Snap and Crop

Usually taken with a camera phone, it sees you and a mate on a night out, pressing your faces together with gormless grins on them. This is the shot that's better suited for Facebook than a professional profile – especially as trying to crop your friend's face out can leave you looking like you've an unfortunate growth on the side of your head (see my previous comment).

The Time Warp

Unless your name is Dorian Grey you're probably not getting any younger, so face up to it. It's delusional to upload a photo of you from another era; if people check you out before meeting you and expect a full mane of glossy hair, but get a balding bonce instead, they're going to know in an instant they can't trust your brand. Even if you've used a current photo, don't forget to make sure in a few years' time that it's still a decent likeness.

The Group Shot

This usually appears when someone's been at an industry event and a professional photographer has been snapping away. The person's grabbed their colleagues, they've all said "Cheese" and the photo has landed in their inbox the next morning. They think 'Great, I need a professional photo for my profile' and use it, leaving us to wonder which one of the group they actually are. Duh!

The Invisible Man

I can't decide if this is better or worse than having a bad photo –

having no photo at all (or the ultimate sin: having your company logo). Either way it's a missed opportunity for people to connect with you and when people buy people, that's important.

SAY MORE THAN "CHEESE!"

Now you know what not to do, let's look at a different type of gallery – one that shows you how thinking about what you want to get across about your brand before you say "Cheese!" can really pay dividends.

Look back at your personal brand pyramid and remind yourself of the relevant ingredients you want to convey (they'll often be sitting in your Behaviours). With those in mind, think about how you would convey that through your facial expression, pose, clothing and backdrop – all the things people will be spotting in your photo. To show you what I mean, here are some examples of profile photos that, while technically the same in that they're head and shoulder shots, are entirely different in what they're saying. (Due to printing this book in black and white, you'll have to imagine what they look like in colour):

 The clues of having no tie, slightly tousled hair and head in hand give the impression of a brand that is casual, laid-back and happy-go-lucky. (More formal people might read the clues as too casual, too fun or too happy-go-lucky.)

 The clues of having hands folded, a knowing smile and a steely gaze give the impression of a brand that has self-assurance, authority and gravitas. (She may be a granny but I don't think she'll be baking a cake for the Women's Institute any time soon!)

The clues from having an unconventional image, hard stare and Mona Lisa smile give the impression of a brand that is enigmatic, strong and individual. (Of course you could also read it as she's a two-faced, mardy, pain in the backside!)

The clues given by having the head tilted back, laughing, in a shot that looks as if it was taken off the cuff give the impression of a brand that is humorous, fun and relaxed. (Or it's someone who'd be cracking naff jokes all the time!)

The clues that come from the tilted head, gentle smile and neutral clothing give the impression of a brand that is a good listener, empathetic and caring. (However, this might all be a bit bland for some people's liking.)

The clues from having the finger on the temple – pointing at the brain – penetrating stare and only the vaguest hint of a smile give the impression of a brand that is intellectual, knowing and reflective (and some might say a little smug).

And a final example...

The clues from this photo of looking over the glasses with a wry smile and sparkling eyes gives the impression of a brand that is clever, witty and doesn't take themself too seriously. (They might also have a sarcastic quip or two up their sleeve).

Whatever opinion you've formed from looking at those photos, the crux of the matter is the facial expressions, pose, clothing and backdrop were all giving you clues to that person's brand. So work out what you want people to know about you and get that across loud and clear.

If you want some inspiration, check out some of the business portraits on photography sites like www.istock.com or www.corbisimages.com. See which ones appeal to you (and therefore to your brand) and download the free samples to guide you – and your photographer – in what you're going for.

TIME FOR YOUR CLOSE-UP

Getting a professional to take your photo is worth the money and if you go in with the samples of what you want your shot to look like you'll have an excellent chance of getting it. Being vague about the end product or leaving the photographer to guess what brand you want to convey is a recipe for disaster.

At the very least, if your budget won't stretch to a pro, find a friend who has a decent camera and ask for their help. Under no circumstances try to take your own picture using the camera on your laptop or iPad – those snaps have a habit of making people look like a photo-fit on *Crimewatch*.

LOAD 'EM UP

Remember: the aim of your photo is to help to make a personal connection with the viewer, even if you're not there. To do that people need to see the whites of your eyes so once you've uploaded your photo use the crop function – and don't be scared to go in tight. Cropping a bit off the top of your head or the side of your shoulder is no bad thing (although don't do what I saw once which was someone who had cropped half her face – I think she was going for 'creative' as her brand but instead ended up with 'psycho').

As an aside, if you want to Photoshop your pic to smooth out a few wrinkles and brighten your smile, I don't have a problem with that (I'll happily admit my forehead has more lines in real-life than it does in on this book-jacket). Don't go mad though…make sure people could still pick you out in a line-up.

One final thing about photos: as consistency is a huge part of promoting your personal brand, consider using the same image for each of your online profiles – LinkedIn, Twitter, website, even your email signature. If you do choose to use different ones, avoid swapping them too often; people get used to looking out for your mugshot in their updates and if you suddenly use an alternative they might not spot it.

Some Dos and Don'ts about Profile Photos

- **DO** always have a photo with your profile – people want to see what you look like.
- **DO** have a photo where you look pretty much as you would if you were to meet in person and **DON'T** use your wedding/holiday/night out snaps.
- **DO** use a professional photographer but **DON'T** let them dictate how you look.
- **DO** prepare some ideas beforehand to show how you want to get across clues to your brand through your clothing, pose, facial expression, background, etc.
- **DO** crop in close so people can see the whites of your eyes.

LINKEDIN

Of all the places you could have an online presence for business, LinkedIn should be your first choice. Not only will you be joining the millions of people already on there, you'll be improving your Google results when someone searches for your name – which I guarantee they will. I've already covered what you need to know about setting up the profile itself, so this bit is about leveraging the other gizmos on offer to really get your personal brand across.

I AM NOT A NUMBER

When you think about what you want to achieve for you or your business, and how you might achieve that, I'd bet my right arm it will be your network of contacts who help you do it. So using LinkedIn to keep in touch with those people – and in turn be connected to the people they know – makes perfect sense.

For some people, LinkedIn is all about the numbers; they hook up with anyone and everyone, figuring the more people they're connected to the bigger their overall network and the greater the pool of people to do business with. I get that...but I don't agree with it.

If you are just a name in someone's address book, with no relationship to back that up, the value of those numbers falls. It's about quality, not quantity, and for people to buy people (the whole tenet of personal branding) it's going to take more than a one-click invitation to deliver the goods.

THE BEST 30 SECONDS YOU EVER SPENT

Let me ask you a question: if you were at an event and saw someone you really wanted to know, who could do wonders for your business or career, would you just walk up to them, hand over your business card and walk away without a word of explanation?

I'm sincerely hoping your answer is "No" but if you've ever sent a LinkedIn invitation and left the message as the standard wording 'I'd like to add you to my professional network' that's exactly what you've done. Not only are you showing how little you value the other person (they weren't even worth 30 seconds of your time personalising the message) you've missed a great opportunity to start building a relationship. Plus you could have got across something about your brand: that you believe in being personal.

Beware of using the LinkedIn app from your phone, or clicking 'connect' in search results for someone's name, as it doesn't allow you to personalise the message before it gets sent. (Though if you do, you can still drop the person a separate email to back it up.) It's only when you're on the main LinkedIn site, with the person's full profile in front of you, that clicking 'connect' allows you to add your own message.

It's definitely worth the extra 30 seconds because, when you think about all the invitations you've had and how few were personalised, you realise how easy it is to stand out from the crowd.

Here are five tips on how you personalise your message:

Tip #1 – Include a salutation

The invitation is an email, so like any other email you should start with a chatty intro to match your personal brand. (There are plenty to choose from in the chapter on emails.)

Tip #2 – Explain where you got their name from

If you don't already know the person, give some background about why you're approaching them: 'I saw you give a presentation at the Tech Conference last week.'

Tip #3 – Explain why you're getting in touch

Making your invitation relevant will definitely help as you're showing you've thought about the mutual benefits: 'I've checked out your profile and notice we work with the same group of people.'

Tip #4 – Suggest a further action

This is usually a way for you to take the relationship further and make it more valuable for both of you: 'I'm in your neck of the woods next Thursday and wondered if you're free for a quick coffee.'

Tip #5 – Include some insight into your personal brand

Subtly give clues to what makes you tick: 'I get a buzz out of connecting people so if you're coming to the next Tech Conference and would like to meet my CEO, just let me know.'

It may take more time to type a personalised message than simply hitting the send button, but it could be the best 30 seconds you ever spent. The value of forming a relationship and not just a connection will ultimately deliver because you'll have someone who has bought into your personal brand and that's worth more than clocking up another contact.

YOU DON'T HAVE TO SAY "I DO"

Just because you're courteous enough to personalise your invitations, not everyone will. You'll undoubtedly get requests that leave you thinking 'Who the heck are you?' and though you might feel obliged to hit 'Accept', that may not be a good idea.

You're judged by the company you keep (remember Kelly Blazek on page 179?) so in those situations I recommend checking out the person's profile to see what value there might be in connecting. Then choose the 'Reply – don't accept yet' option and ask for more information, something along the lines of: 'Thanks for your invitation. I don't believe we've met (although I could be wrong – my memory's not what it used to be) so was interested in your thoughts on wanting to connect.'

By asking them their reasoning, you often find opportunities arising in a way they wouldn't if you'd accepted without any further details.

Here's what I'm talking about...
Having received a bog-standard invitation from a lady named Joanne, I replied to find out more. She sent a message saying she'd seen me speak at a conference so had taken a look at my profile, hitting 'connect' with the intention of simply following my updates. However, as I'd taken the time to drop her a line, she explained she was interested in working with me and, long story short, became my client.

Sometimes though, you can get an answer you didn't expect...

Here's what I'm talking about...
A guy I'd never met or even heard of sent me a standard invitation. When I replied asking why he wanted to connect he explained he was a single man looking for someone who believed in a one woman/one man relationship, had seen my profile, thought I fitted the bill and wanted to know more about me, so could we have a chat. I replied to say he was correct, that I was a one woman/one man gal, but as I'd already found my man and been with him over 20 years I probably wasn't the lass he was looking for!

LET'S GET INTRODUCED

A lot of the value of LinkedIn lies in its ability to make connections with people you don't yet know but would definitely like to. There's a lot to be said for spending some time looking at who your connections are connected to, especially if you have a good enough relationship with them to ask for an introduction.

You can of course take the impersonal route to doing that, choosing 'Get introduced' from the online options then filling in the messages to both the person you'd like to meet and the person you have in common (the one who'll be doing the intro). There's a possible pitfall to that though. If your contact doesn't know the other person well you may have put them in an awkward position; they wouldn't feel comfortable introducing you to someone they don't really know, but think you may take it personally if they refuse your request.

The way to avoid that, and give yourself a chance to strengthen your existing relationship, is to give your contact a bell. Ring them up, have a natter, catch up on old times, then ask, "By the way...I was looking on LinkedIn and noticed you're connected to [insert name of potential contact here]. How well do you know them?"

Their answer might be "Not well" but even then it could lead them to ask why you want to get introduced and from that they could come up with other people to connect you with. If their answer is "Really well" ask them if they'd be happy to introduce you.

Here's what I'm talking about...

Browsing LinkedIn one day, I noticed I was indirectly connected to a leadership development manager via my former client, Martin. As I already work with a lot of L&D people, I decided to give Martin a ring to find out more. After catching up on his news and telling him mine I asked how well he knew the person in question. He replied that James was a good friend but he hadn't seen him in ages, could do with arranging a coffee and that he'd invite me along. He did just that and the result was I'm now working with James' company. I doubt that would have happened if I'd used LinkedIn's email system to ask for the introduction.

When asking someone for an introduction, it's important to stress that if they'd rather not, that would be absolutely fine because you value the fact their reputation is involved and they need to feel comfortable aligning that with you. (After all, I'm sure you can think of times you've been asked to make an introduction but haven't rated the person asking so have felt put on the spot.)

To make the other person's job as matchmaker even easier, offer to send them a brief email saying why you'd like to meet the other person (including why it would be beneficial to them to hook up). Your contact can simply forward it on with a personal note, saving them time and effort, plus you've made sure you've described who you are and what you do in the way you want.

Once you've been introduced and the ball is rolling on your new relationship, there's an important thing to remember: drop the person who introduced you a line to let them know how it's going and thank them for their part in that. Not only is it good manners, it's another chance to stay on their radar and will go a long way to endearing you to them should you need another blind date. If their introduction turns into something big, like a new job or a contract, a more tangible thank you is the way to go; a bunch of flowers or bottles of wine never go amiss (well, not in my house).

MAY I RECOMMEND...?

People tend to have split views on the value of having recommendations on your profile. Some think it's all a sham, that the comments come from sycophantic mates and carry as much truth as an MP's expenses claim. Others, me included, think they add an extra bit of insight, especially if it's clear they're from clients or credible contacts and not just colleagues. If you're job-hunting, they're definitely a benefit as surveys show recruiters see them as a positive addition.

You may not feel comfortable asking for a recommendation – after all, the person might say "No" (ouch) – but if you're going about it the right way there's every chance they'll say "Yes" (which would do your confidence no end of good).

Firstly, you need to consider who to solicit your recommendations from because credibility is key. Only ask contacts who you can say, hand on heart, you've worked for or with, so they have first-hand experience of what you deliver. Be wary of asking anyone who has worked for you, because if you've paid for their services that could be seen as swaying their response.

Secondly, you need to personalise your recommendation request; you're asking the person to give their valuable time penning a testimonial, so the least you can do is spend some of your valuable time asking for it. This time though, I'd advise getting in touch via email as it gives the other person some breathing space before replying. Aligning their reputation with yours for an introduction is one thing, using it to wave the flag for you is another, so they have to feel confident it won't come back and bite them. Remember to keep your language positive (which can be hard if you're looking for a job and your confidence has taken a knock) and you'll increase your chances of getting what you need.

Here's what I'm talking about...

I once received a recommendation request from a woman I knew reasonably well but had never worked with. We hadn't seen each other for years but she was getting in touch because, "I very reluctantly have to get a move on with finding another job, so here I am biting the bullet and doing this awful, embarrassing thing of asking people I know to recommend me." What's your perception of her words? I knew this woman had been great at her job but what was coming over was incredibly negative. I understood why (looking for a job is stressful and she had my utmost sympathy) but it wasn't something I wanted to align myself with so I deleted the request.

Some people find writing recommendations a doddle. For others, composing a few lines is akin to filling in their tax return – it should be easy but they know it'll turn into a headache.

Although you don't want to dictate what the person puts you can help them get started by saying why you want the recommendation ('I'm trying to create a comprehensive LinkedIn profile because I'm looking for a new job'). What sort of things you'd like covered are also good ('It would be great if you could include something about my technical skills and the contribution they made to delivering projects.')

And once you have the recommendation, you will of course send a thank you note to the person in question (your mother brought you up with manners, didn't she?)

A word of warning though: although a string of recommendations can certainly boost the power of you profile, having too many can tip into overkill – especially if some of them have been around longer than Bruce Forsyth. So use the 'Manage recommendations' function to keep things in check.

...OR AT LEAST ENDORSE?

Endorsements are another way for people to acknowledge your skills. However, as they're so quick and easy to give, they lack the kudos of a recommendation. (I've had complete strangers endorsing my skills.)

There are some upsides though: when you endorse someone they get a notification, so it's a good way to get back onto their radar. Plus if the person replies to say thank you, it provide another opportunity to strengthen your relationship. And when you receive an endorsement, dropping the person a line to say thank you does the same thing.

WASSUP? LET ME TELL YOU

Once you've got your profile sussed and your personal brand is coming across loud and clear, you'll have every right to feel a little smug; you've just achieved what so many users haven't. To keep up the good work and stay on people's radars, the next step is to use the 'Share an update' function regularly. That means when your connections get their LinkedIn updates showing what you've been up to you'll have something more exciting than the fact you've accepted an invitation. (The message 'John Smith is now connected to...' becomes 10mph wallpaper very quickly.)

The 9½mph thing to do is to use the updates, either on your individual profile or within a group, to:

- share your expertise (if you write a blog or have had an article published, put it up)
- share others' expertise (if you read an interesting story or see a great presentation, put it up)
- share events (if you're holding one of your own or going to someone else's, put it up)
- share tips (if you've discovered a useful bit of info, or read an outstanding book put it up)
- share views (if you have an opinion, put it up)
- ask for others' views (if you have a question, put it up)

Be sure to add a comment as to why you're sharing your update. (Just pasting a link and leaving it at that isn't adding real value.) Not only will you create a positive online presence, you'll get yourself noticed in your contacts' inboxes.

JOB HUNTING

If you're looking for a job, LinkedIn should be your new best friend because more and more recruitment agencies are using it to source candidates, while more and more companies are using it to bypass the recruiters and fill their vacancies directly. To come to their attention, it's worth slipping a few extra key words into your profile copy (key words being the ones recruiters will put into LinkedIn's search engine). Good places to do that include your headline (the line that appears under your name) and in each of the job descriptions you list in your experience. You can even customise your profile's url (the web address that takes people to your page) to slip the odd one in there too.

Another option is to make it clear in your headline that you're on the market, using phrases like 'looking for a position in [specific sector] and open to opportunities' or 'Seeking a [job title] position, particularly in [specific sector]'. (Some recruiters have said they like this as it makes their job easier, however, others have said they prefer to find people who are less likely to be on other recruiters' radars, so it's your call.)

Making sure your contact details are current is also a must so people can get hold of you when they find you. It may seem obvious but if you've just left your last place of employment, you could well still have your old email address listed.

Some Dos and Don'ts about LinkedIn

- **DO** get your profile on LinkedIn – it's the #1 business networking site and prime advertising space for your brand.
- **DON'T** use the standard copy for any invitations, introductions or recommendations but **DO** take time to personalise your message.
- **DON'T** just accept an invitation, especially if it's using the standard wording, but **DO** use it as an opportunity to find out more.
- **DO** post regular updates to build a positive presence and keep you on people's radars.
- **DO** include key words that are relevant to your sector if you're looking for a job.

TWITTER

Twitter is another great way to keep in touch. It takes seconds
to post a message of your own or respond to other people's
(especially worthwhile if they're one of your A Listers). It's also a
great place to make contact with people you wouldn't normally be
able to...which brings some great opportunities.

Here's what I'm talking about...

A friend of mine had started her PR career with an agency in
Manchester but wanted to move on. She had her eye on another
agency that had an award-winning reputation but, because of that,
would be hard to get into. She began following the agency's CEO
on Twitter, reading his posts, re-tweeting some, then eventually
dropping him a line to say she'd love a chance to work with him.
He put her in touch with his HR team, they met for a chat and she
ended up as an account exec within six months.

I'm a fan of Twitter – but that doesn't mean you have to be.
I've lost count of the times I've heard the words, "I need to start
tweeting," and when I've asked the person why they've replied,
"Because everyone else is," or "I've been told I should." As I said at
the beginning of this chapter, only use the online media that will
reach the people you want to buy your brand and even then, only
do it if you can do it well.

WHAT'S YOUR HANDLE?

Like an email address (see page 108), your Twitter name can give
a host of clues to who you are, so choose wisely. As the service is
used in nearly every country in the world, getting a handle that
matches your name exactly is unlikely, unless you have an unusual
spelling. Play around with using an underscore (one of these: _) or
your initials, or your company name, or a relevant alias until you
find something that works.

When you're setting up your profile you also have the opportunity to include a 160 character description – 20 characters longer than your tweets. As Twitter is a more social place than LinkedIn, feel free to be more personal and a bit quirkier. (Don't go too far though; I was once followed by a youngster whose profile told me he was 'a bit of a c**t' – only he didn't use asterisks!)

If you have an engaging profile that conveys your professional and personal side, people will assume you write engaging tweets and be more likely to follow you. For example, my profile reads:

@SparkBranding: Author of Personal Branding for Brits, I help people blow their own trumpets without sounding like an eejit then relax and sip Rioja as I listen to The Archers.

Some others I like are:

- @duncanbury: Founder of Miascape. I'm a bald guy and an independent thinker (some say I'm Bruce Willis with a PhD) encouraging people in business to think for themselves.

- @nat_silverton: Beauty journo of 15 years. Mother of two, wife of one, lover of lipstick.

- @sparklyscotty: Compulsive learner and geek. Typical digital marketer mix of a statistician's head, a writer's soul and a puppy's happy enthusiasm.

- @steverake: Director at Harvey Nash. Sports enthusiast, seasoned real ale drinker, amateur boxer and terrible dancer.

Another thing to consider is your Twitter pic that goes with the summary. Again, you can be a bit quirkier than you can on LinkedIn, although there's a lot to be said for having the same picture so people can instantly spot you wherever they come across you online. What you shouldn't do though is use a company logo. People are buying people and want to know it's a person who's behind the messages, so get your ugly mug out there!

GET CHIRPING

Once you've set up your Twitter account you need to have a strategy for what you're going to say. Without one you could end up with ramblings that waste both your and your followers' time.

A statistic from one American report said that only 36% of all the tweets on Twitter are of any interest to users, while 25% of them are actively disliked – especially if they contain an over-use of #hashtags. The rest are ignored entirely, like a middle-aged man with a sagging paunch and chronic halitosis at a singles night.

When you take a look at what's being launched into the Twittersphere, it's hardly surprising there's little to excite the reader. A quick glance online had me regaled with such bon mots as: 'Note to self: don't go for a run first thing in the morning without breakfast' (if the note is to yourself why share it with others?), 'Tidied my office yesterday in readiness for a visitor. He's not coming now but I like my tidy desk' (is that the epitome of a non-event?) and 'Hmm, phone battery down to 80% already – think I need to swap to a new one' (genius).

THE SFW RULE

It's time to apply the SFW Rule, created by one of my clients to test the value of every one of his company's communications by asking the question, "So flipping what?" (Well, that's what I presumed the 'F' stands for.) If a good answer can't be given, the message doesn't go out.

That isn't to say the odd bit of trivia doesn't add value to your brand – it does because it lets people know you're human. Just don't make it the entire focus of your messages otherwise you'll come across as me, me, me...and that's not what social media is all about. Here's a guide to the types of tweets you should be doing, based on advice from Mark Shaw (@markshaw), a guru on the subject:

Tweet type #1 – Sharing information

These tweets are about spreading the reach of things you have found valuable that others might too – links to blogs (yours and others'), product recommendations, discount offers, other people's tweets. This sends clues about your personal brand that you're interested in things other than yourself.

Tweet type #2 – Engaging with people

This is about showing you're 'listening' as you respond to tweets others have posted, answering questions and giving advice to establish your credentials. The result is you boost your personal brand by being seen as an expert in your field as well as someone who's willing to give your time helping others.

Tweet type #3 – Social chit chat

You can also engage with people in a social way, responding to their tweets and having a bit of banter (though if the conversation goes on too long it can lose its appeal for anyone else reading). As I showed you with the earlier examples though, listing the minutiae of your life can quickly become dull, unless you're a celebrity who lives in a bubble of glamour.

Here's what I'm talking about...

When Lady Gaga tweets, "Looking forward to shooting my parfum commercial with Steven Klein," it holds a certain amount of interest (though being the curmudgeon I am I couldn't care less). When you tweet, "Taking my dog to the park – hope it doesn't rain!" the interest factor is somewhat less.

Bottom line: if you're not sure if your tweet is worth chirping, ask yourself "SFW?"

THE DAWN CHORUS

The last piece of advice I have to offer about Twitter concerns how often you tweet. Too much and you'll come across as someone with nothing better to do, too little and your little blips won't even register on people's radars.

There's no hard and fast rule on quantities but however many messages you're sending it's a good idea to space them out over the course of the day. You can either do that in real time, tapping away on your mobile as you go about your business, or you can schedule them using some of the free services like Twitter itself or www.hootsuite.com.

I do the latter, spending half an hour on a Sunday going through my diary for the coming week, setting up two or three tweets for each day about who I'm meeting or where I'm going, perhaps dropping in a bit of social chit chat and the odd link to my blog. I then add to them with ad hoc tweets as things come up or as I respond to others' messages. Plus when I'm reading interesting things on the internet I'll use www.bufferapp.com (another free service) to create a pool of tweets ready to be sent at timed intervals.

Some Dos and Don'ts about Twitter
- **DON'T** use Twitter just because "everyone else is".
- **DO** remember it's a more social site than LinkedIn so you can be a bit quirkier.
- **DO** get the balance of your tweets right: share information, engage with people, have some chit chat.
- **DON'T** think your life is as interesting as Lady Gaga's – it's not.
- **DO** consider using a mix of scheduled and ad hoc tweets to give a rounded picture.

FACEBOOK

Facebook is the last of the 'big three' online channels. Sitting at the other end of the spectrum from LinkedIn with its business focus, Facebook is definitely about the social side of your brand. I'll be honest and say I don't use it because: a) my day job is business-to-business, not business-to-consumer, so LinkedIn is the place for me; b) as Facebook is a social channel you need to have the time to be sociable, replying to comments and having conversations, which I don't; and c) I'm just not into it.

If you're in the same boat, feel free to ignore Facebook too. However, if your business is more consumer-focused and you have the time and resource to connect with people, use it to your advantage. People buy people here more than anywhere so getting your personality out there, not hiding behind your company, is a must. Keep in mind what you want to share and what's best left in the vault though (remember the ladder on page 67?)

Here's what I'm talking about...
Picture the scene: a young woman is being interviewed for a position in the PR team of a trendy beauty brand. The interviewer asks, "Are you a party girl?" She's unsure how to reply (she does like to party, but surely she shouldn't admit it) but before she can answer he says, "It certainly looks like it from your Facebook page!" Her initial shock gives way to disbelief that she could have been so stupid as to let any Tom, Dick or Harry see photos of her on her numerous nights out.

That's a true story, told to me by the woman in question after I'd delivered a seminar about promoting your personal brand online. However, her anecdote ended with a twist: the guy had gone on to say, "Because a party girl is just who we're looking for." She struck lucky, but for the remaining 99.99% of us it's bad news for your brand to be too familiar on Facebook.

Of course, you might be reading this and thinking, "But I've got a Facebook page and I don't use it for my business at all – just socially". In which case I have one piece of advice...

KEEP YOUR PRIVATES PRIVATE

Always pay attention to your privacy settings. Forgetting to do that and posting a photo of you dressed as a lady of the night for that tarts and vicars party might lead to some interesting conversations (particularly if you're a burly bloke who's usually sporting a three-piece suit in the boardroom).

It's not just you who could post dodgy photos though – what about all the other people who have taken a snap of you? For that reason you should also set up notifications to flag when other people are posting things about you, so you can try and stay in control of what's online.

Some Dos and Don'ts about Facebook
- **DO** use Facebook if your business focus is business-to-consumer.
- **DON'T** use it if you have little time to be sociable – if you can't engage with people they'll soon go elsewhere.
- **DO** check your privacy settings are as they should be.
- **DO** set up notifications for any mentions on other people's pages.

BLOGS AND NEWSLETTERS

If you want to stay in touch with your A Listers and build your reputation as someone who's an expert in your field, you might consider writing a blog or newsletter...but only if you have something to say. Before hitting the keys, make sure you have a precise objective for what you want to achieve because wittering on about nothing in particular just because "it's about time I sent another update" will get you a reputation as a spammer who's best ignored.

Don't forget though: this is as much about getting across your personal brand as what you have to talk about; people will enjoy reading what you have to say if they know there's a real person behind the words. It's a prime time to write as you speak so keep your language chatty and be sure to drop in the odd ingredient from your pyramid and relationship hooks too. Remember to tell stories that will stick in people's minds (page 167) and you can't go wrong chucking in the odd 'because...' (page 120).

PLAN, PLAN, PLAN

When I began blogging the best bit of advice I received was from online media expert Michaela Laubscher from Social Alchemy. She recommended planning a timetable of what I'd write about in my blogs and I suggest you do the same (ditto if you email a newsletter). Sit down with a piece of paper or type up a list of all the things you talk to people about when you're discussing your area of expertise. Think about conversations you've had and pinpoint the titbits that really got your listener's attention. Think about presentations you've delivered and the questions you got afterwards. Think about clients you've worked with and the problems they faced. Think about things that are going on in the news and how they're relevant. Think about what you'd say if you had to explain what you do to a seven year old.

Get it all out of your head and down in black and white, then arrange your ideas into some sort of coherent order that your readers can follow. (A friend of mine chose the letters of the alphabet to give his weekly blogs a theme.) Congratulations… you now have a plan.

What you have to decide next is how often you're going to post your blog/email your newsletter. Be realistic. There's no point saying you'll write something every other day when, a month in, you're struggling for time and give up; it sends a negative message if people look online and see you haven't uploaded anything new for months.

Set the frequency to match your workloads, then stick to it, and if for any reason you can't, manage people's expectations with a quick update to explain why. (If you pitch it right you can even turn this negative into a positive, like the "I'm running late" example on page 127.)

HAVE AN OPINION

The best blogs and newsletters are the ones that make you think – even if what you're thinking is 'I disagree' – so if you have an opinion, state it (all sitting on the fence gets you is splinters in your backside).

Here's what I'm talking about…

I get a lot of newsletters in my inbox but the one I open without fail is from Thor Holt, a guy who helps business people present with confidence. He's an outspoken Scotsman who gets a rush from making people realise they can do more than they ever thought they could, so his updates are full of things to make you think and push you out of your comfort zone. (He's the reason I wrote a list of people I needed to keep in touch with and set about contacting them.) Just as he does in person, he states his opinion and his brand comes across loud and clear.

However, this isn't about saying, "It's my way or the highway." What it is about is inviting people to comment (a great way to end each blog is with a question) so you can find out what they think too, because as I said before, communication is as much about listening as talking. To do that online, you need to make sure you reply to people's comments quickly and make your response personal.

And if forming an opinion from scratch isn't your forte, curating others' views just might be. That means finding interesting content that's been created elsewhere (setting up RSS feeds from a variety of credible sources should do it) then commenting on and sharing it with your audience. It's just as valid if you're adding your voice and it can save you a lot of time.

Plus, if you're someone who wants to raise your profile in your sector, but have shied away from it because you don't consider yourself a great writer, this could be just for you. Even adding short comments to an existing article or blog could still get you seen and read.

WORDS AND PICTURES

As much as the words on the screen, your readers will be getting clues to your brand from the look of your blog or newsletter, so consider how you can convey who you are through the design, images and even typeface you use. There are plenty of free templates out there to get you on your way – particularly if you're using the most common blogging tool wordpress.com – but some are so cheesy they'd give a mountain of Stilton a run for its money, so choose wisely.

Make sure any design you set up includes a photo of you (after all, you're the one with the opinions). Or if you really want people to get the full impact of your personal brand, consider posting video blogs.

YOUTUBE

If you're someone who feels comfortable in front of the camera, YouTube is a great place to build your personal brand (and boost your ratings in Google). You can create your own channel, customise its design, include your photo, add a summary of what you're all about, then start to build a library of videos. They don't just have to be blogs either. 'How to' videos are really popular and if you want to raise your profile as an expert in your field, sharing your knowledge with a quick demo is a good way to go. Remember to produce a quality video to reflect your quality brand though; there are plenty of amateurs out there and you don't want to be labelled as one of them.

Some Dos and Don'ts about Blogs and Newsletters

- **DO** use blogs and newsletters to keep in touch with people on a regular basis and build your credibility...if you have something to say.
- **DO** write with personality, including ingredients from your brand pyramid and relationship hooks.
- **DON'T** leave your blogs or newsletters to chance so you end up wittering on about nothing – it'll do more damage than good.
- **DO** plan what you're going to say and have an opinion when you're saying it.
- **DO** include your photo so people know whose opinion it is.
- **DON'T** go for a cheesy design template.

WEBSITE

And so to the last section on tooting your horn online...your website. No matter who you work for – yourself or a huge corporate beast – there's one thing that should be at the heart of your homepage: human beings. Remember what I said right back at the beginning? People buy people, so make sure you're giving them someone to buy (and if you are your business that should be a no-brainer).

LIGHTS, CAMERA, ACTION!

If you have the budget (and even if you don't but could scrape the money together) video is by far the best thing to have on your website. Instead of having to decipher your brand from the words on the screen, people can see you in action and gather twice as many clues from your tone of voice and body language. However, they'll also pick up clues from the quality and production of the film, so pay a professional or invest in a decent piece of kit before you record your star turn (using your mobile phone does not count). You want to make sure the signals you send are Hollywood blockbuster, not straight-to-DVD flop.

If you want people to watch, you'll need to keep it short and sweet. Video expert Steve Reilly from VistaBee says 90 seconds should be your goal – so preparing a script beforehand brings focus. That's when you should be considering how to include not only one or two key messages about what you do, but also one or two about what you do, because it's your personal brand people will ultimately be buying. If you're talking about what you offer, talk about why you do that (your Drivers). If you're talking about the problems you solve for your customers, talk about the attitude you have when doing it (your Behaviours). If you're talking about the things people can expect from your service, talk about the extras you deliver (your Skills). Your Image should, of course, speak for itself.

ABOUT US

When you visit a company's website, what's one of the first pages you visit? If you're anything like the people I speak to it's the 'About us' page; our urge for buying people, not just products or services, is what makes us click the link. It's mighty disappointing then when you discover loads of copy about the company itself (when it was set up, how many offices it has, what awards it's won) and nowt about the people in it.

Alternatively, you visit the 'Meet the team' page and simply get a list of names and job titles of people who work there – no photo, not biography, nothing.

What people really want is:

- To have enough information to decide then and there if they're buying that person's brand.
- To see what the person in question looks like, with a professionally-taken, well cropped, clue-laden photo.
- To read something about them that gives three key pieces of information: credibility, personal brand and relationship hooks – preferably written in 9½mph language.

Here's what I'm talking about...

Maloco & Associates is a solicitors and estate agency in Dunfermline – so far, so boring. Its website includes a link to 'The Team' and when you click on it you're greeted by individual photos of the people who work there – so far, so normal. Each photo is accompanied by another one of the same person when they were younger – so far, so intriguing. Each childhood pic is accompanied not by the usual biography but by memories of their first record, childhood dream job and favourite TV programme – so far, so brilliant. I don't even live in Scotland and I'd want them to sell my house!

MASTER OF YOU OWN DOMAIN

The ultimate in personal branding is to have your own website that's solely about you, preferably with your name as the web address. That's not always easy – mine was already taken by a newsreader in Florida – but as with your Twitter handle (page 210) you can find alternative ways to set out your name. The site doesn't have to be more than a page or two covering areas like your biography, achievements and personal blog (if you have one) but used alongside your LinkedIn, Twitter and/or Facebook accounts it can boost your online profile even further.

Some Dos and Don'ts about Websites

- **DO** consider investing in a good quality video – it's worth a thousand words because people can see you in action and gather twice as many clues as they can by reading copy.
- **DO** have an 'About us' or 'Meet the team' section that means just that – not more blurb about the company.
- **DON'T** be shy and **DO** consider the ultimate in personal branding: having your own personal website.

YOUR MARKETING PLAN

Phew...who knew there were so many ways you could be promoting yourself? You might even be feeling a little overwhelmed at the prospect of tackling them all. That's where a final bit of thinking can make all the difference – creating a marketing plan for your personal brand.

It works in exactly the same way as a marketing plan for any brand in that there are four key things to consider:

1. What do you want to achieve by using your personal brand? (That's your goal.)
2. Who are the key people you need buy-in from to help you achieve that? (They are your audiences.)
3. What are the ways those people come into contact with you? (Those are your channels.)
4. What do you need those people to know about you? (Those are your messages.)

GET IT DOWN ON PAPER

By setting out the answers to those questions using the page opposite, you start to create your marketing plan. As you will likely have more than one audience for your goal, you'll need to repeat the exercise for each person. For example, if your goal is a promotion, key audience #1 would be the person making the hiring decision, but that person's PA might be key audience #2 (their opinion could hold a lot of sway) and a previous boss who could put in a good word could be key audience #3.

You can download blank copies of the plan (as many as you need) at www.sparkexec.co.uk/personal-branding-for-brits. Don't forget to revisit and revise your plan as you achieve your goals and set new ones.

What is your goal (short, medium or long-term)?

Who is a key person you need buy-in from to achieve that?
Who would it help to have as an advocate for your brand?

What are their key motivators? What matters to them?

What aspect of your personal brand appeals to those motivators?
What do you offer that would be good for them to know about?

What are the key ways they come into contact with you?
What opportunities do you have to communicate with them?

What message do you need to get across about your brand?
What clues can you give your audiences via those channels?

YOU'RE ON THE HOME STRAIGHT

Congratulations! You've made it to the end of the book and now it's time for you to set out into the big, wide world of personal branding. Before you do, I'd like to act like the 'proud mother' I am and give you some final tips to keep you on the right path – what I call my 10 Commandments of Personal Brand. Don't worry, I'm not going to go all Moses on you and decree how to lead a wholesome life. (If you want to covet your neighbour's ass, go ahead – but don't blame me when it all goes pear-shaped!)

THE 10 COMMANDMENTS

#1 – Be true

The bottom line is if you can't believe in the personal brand you're peddling, you can't expect anyone else to either. Being authentic is the lynchpin of your brand and that means being yourself – warts and all. (So long as there's not more warts than good bits, in which case you'll be needing the number of a good therapist.)

#2 – Be clear

Now you have your brand, clarity will help people to understand what you have to offer. That means keeping focused and not being afraid to repeat your brand messages. After all, Nike has been saying 'Just Do It' for decades without blurring the message by adding 'Get a move on', 'Shake a leg' or 'Pull your finger out'.

#3 – Be consistent

This commandment ties in directly with #1 and #2 because as well as being authentic and clear you need to be consistent, making sure you deliver in everything you say and do, talking the talk and walking the walk (or as 80s popstrel Betty Boo would sing, "Doing the do".)

#4 – Take aim

This commandment is about having a clear idea of who you want to buy into your brand and how you come into contact with them. Don't waste time on Twitter or Facebook if that's not where your audience lies; focus your efforts where they will see and hear what you have to offer.

#5 – Don't stop

Consumer brands don't advertise their product once and expect people to buy it – they keep repeating their ads knowing it takes time for the message to make an impact. It's the same for your personal brand. You need to keep it updated, adding or deleting stuff as your career changes, staying on people's radars so they'll know where to find you when the time's right.

#6 – Say something

Think about it…when you met someone for the first time, what was the thing you remembered about them? Their job title and company name, or that amusing anecdote they told you about that time they saw Lorraine Kelly with her bra off? (Which is an actual story I was told by a former client of mine.) So say something engaging!

#7 – Understand how your brand is perceived

Having taken the time to find out how others see your personal brand (don't tell me you skipped that chapter) there's a lot to be said for occasionally repeating the feedback exercise, even in an informal way, to make sure you're still on track.

#8 – Be simple

Having honed your brand don't be tempted to broaden it out again; our natural instinct is to make sure we offer as much as possible to appeal to as many people as possible, but as I tell my clients, "Let's keep focused on the good shit." Which ties in with...

#9 – One for all

When companies do their branding, they often create separate brands for different audiences, like supermarkets differentiating their 'value' and 'luxury' ranges. That's not possible for your personal brand (what would happen if you met your 'value' and 'luxury' audiences at the same time?) Stay in one ballpark then make sure you play out of your socks!

#10 – Be unique

In business today, finding a true unique selling point (USP) for what you have to offer is like finding me taking out gym membership – it may happen one day but I wouldn't hold your breath waiting. Celebrate the fact the only real USP you have is you.

Here endeth the sermon.

Don't forget...
Want to share your thoughts on this book? Or sign up for my blog to receive more personal brand tips? Drop me a line at jennifer.holloway@sparkexec.co.uk or visit www.sparkexec.co.uk

And if you'd really like to help me spread the word, please hurry over to Amazon right now and write a review. Thank you!

A FEW THANK YOUS

I'm not big on schmaltz but I am big on manners so there are a few thank yous I'd like to make. First up is Philip Dearing, the man who mentored me in the early days of my business, giving me the necessary kick up the proverbial when warranted and pat on the back when earned. Second is Alan Halsall, my current mentor, who acts as my cheerleader and keeps me on track. Heather Church also played her part – a South-African who showed me you could be positive about yourself without being arrogant.

My designer Mark Spanton gave me a book-jacket to be proud of and photographer Mark Ingram helped bring it to life, plus Cat Hepple snapped my author picture.

Jason McKeown and Gilvray Croudson knocked my ramblings into shape, Sue Gittins helped me find a way through the publishing maze, plus numerous authors shared their words of wisdom, including Barrie Hopson, Andy McMenemy and in particular Heather Townsend.

Thanks also to the people who appeared as case studies, either with or without their identities, and the ones who have been faithfully reading (and commenting on) my blogs for years; your feedback spurred me on and gave me the confidence to write this book.

ABOUT THE AUTHOR

 When it comes to personal branding, Jennifer Holloway knows her stuff. From her corporate days running press offices to being the boss of her own business she's built relationships, gained clients and stayed on people's radars by promoting who she is – not just what she does.

As the author of *Personal Branding For Brits*, she's taken what she's learnt and created a practical guide to blowing your own trumpet to help as many people as possible discover being successful means being yourself. (Even if that's admitting you're a fan of *The Archers* like she is!)

Jennifer first experienced the benefits of promoting a personal brand when she worked with the media. By getting journalists to buy into her, not just her stories, she garnered front page headlines and appearances on *The Today Programme*, *BBC Breakfast* and *Sky News*. Then when she made the tough decision to go it alone and launch Spark, her personal brand became the epitome of what she was selling.

As well as her knack for spotting someone's USP and talent for bringing their brand to life, Jennifer offers another valuable service: straight-talking honesty. Her sassy style is suited to those who like a challenge and are driven to keep moving forwards (just as she is).

Jennifer loves to talk about personal brand whether that's delivering speeches to large audiences, running workshops for smaller groups or helping people one-to-one. (Her clients include Microsoft, Asda, RBS, Arla, KPMG, Barclays, Hallmark and Coutts.) She's been told her 'double espresso' enthusiasm is so contagious she leaves her audiences' heads buzzing with ideas to instantly improve their brands.

 Jennifer balances being in the limelight by living her version of *The Good Life* in the Yorkshire Dales: pottering around the garden in her wellies, keeping bees and feeding chickens, then ending the day with a well-deserved glass of Rioja.

Working with Jennifer...
If you're curious about how personal branding could work for you or your organisation, get in touch via jennifer.holloway@sparkexec.co.uk

TESTIMONIALS FOR JENNIFER

"I really enjoyed Jennifer's infectious laughter, no-frills attitude and great results. I'd recommend her to anyone struggling with their brand."
Miha Kralj, Senior Technology Director, Microsoft

"Jennifer's not afraid to give an honest opinion and really challenges people, all the while reinforcing their self-confidence."
Jo Smedley, Leadership Development Manager, Arla

"The workshop was valuable. I'm seeing improved engagement, an appreciation of alternative points of view, self reflection, plus an improved awareness of self and style in the fullest sense."
Will Smith, Construction & Facilities Director, Asda

"It was extremely thought provoking material, relevant to everyone and has given me plenty to think about. Needless to say, I have been sure to recommend it to all the 'sceptics' I work with."
Alan Peabody, Senior Director, RBS

"Jennifer is witty and insightful and helped me crystallise the values that were important to gain satisfaction in my career."
Max Pell, Managing Director, XChanging

INDEX